Effective Coaching

Myles Downey

TEXERE

New York • London

Copyright © 1999, 2001, 2002, 2003 by Myles Downey

The right of Myles Downey to be identified as the
author of this work has been asserted by him in accordance with the
Copyright, Designs and Patents Act 1988.

First published in Great Britain in 1999 by
Orion Business

Reprinted in 2002, 2003
Published in 2001 by
TEXERE Publishing Limited
71-77 Leadenhall Street
London EC3A 3DE
Tel: +44 (0)20 7204 3644
Fax: +44 (0)20 7208 6701
www.etexere.co.uk

A subsidiary of
TEXERE LLC
55 East 52nd Street
New York, NY 10055
Tel: +1 (212) 317 5511
Fax: +1 (212) 317 5178
www.etexere.com

A CIP catalogue record for this book
is available from the British Library

ISBN: 1-58799-120-9

Printed and bound in Great Britain by
Cox & Wyman Ltd, Reading, Berkshire

Acknowledgments

This book was made possible by the coaches, mentors and teachers I have been privileged to know. To these people I owe infinite thanks; Alan Fine, Graham Alexander, Sir John Whitmore, Susie Morell, Ben Cannon, Caroline Harris, Charles Sherno, Chris Morgan and Philip Goldman. I am grateful too, to my colleagues at The School of Coaching at The Industrial Society, in particular Tony Morgan, Peter Hill and Jane Meyler. And a final word of thanks to Tim Gallwey for writing *The Inner Game of Tennis*, a book that opened up a new world for me.

Contents

Introduction

The primary aim of this book is to present a comprehensive introduction to effective coaching in business; from an understanding of what coaching is, to an insight into the key models and skills, to clear description of the applications. If you are intent on learning to coach then I believe this is a good place to start.

The second aim is a bit more challenging – for the author at least. Work for many people is something to be put up with. For some it is drudgery and boredom, for others stress and pressure. It pays the mortgage or makes other pleasures possible. Obviously this is not true for everyone and even for those for whom it is true there may be some satisfaction to be had, some special friendships and the occasional success. But try this test. Ask people what they would do if they did not have to work. Ask yourself. Most people would choose to do something different. Work is not where most people go for fulfilment (although this is changing in some more far-sighted organisations). What a tragedy. What a waste to spend eight hours a day, five days a week in the pursuit of . . . nothing.

I believe that work can be productive, fulfilling and a joy. Productive in that people can pursue and achieve results that make extraordinary demands of them, fulfilling in that it has meaning and encourages learning and personal development. And joy. Coaching is a big part of what it takes to achieve these ends. So the second aim of this book is to inspire you to become a great coach.

However, you will not learn to coach by reading this book. You will not even develop a significant level of skill. I think you should be clear about that at the outset. Learning to coach requires, amongst other things, a lot of practice, feedback and supervision and a book can provide none of these. If this book informs you and inspires you its job is done.

The book has been written for a number of audiences. The primary group is composed of managers in organisations who are looking for more effective ways of working with colleagues. They are aware that the more traditional approaches to managing people are becoming less and less appropriate. They are probably beginning to realise that the kinds of behaviours that have made them successful as managers in the past may now be getting in the way of their own progress – and that of their staff.

The second group is composed of people who see that their role in work, or a large part of it, is to coach others, for example management development specialists or internal consultants.

Finally this book is for anyone, from teachers to parents to sports coaches, who is inspired to help others, either personally or professionally, in having their work or play be productive, fulfilling and a joy.

In the early eighties the word coaching did not appear in the business lexicon and the practice was virtually unheard of, although I am sure that it was happening. When I think of the people, in all walks of life, who have really helped me learn or give my best, I now realise they all demonstrated some of the attributes of great coaches. That may have been a willingness to listen to my point of view or opinion or it may be that they caused me to explore an issue in greater depth. But the point remains that back then coaching was not formally acknowledged as a part of management. This has changed quite dramatically. Now, at the end of the nineties, the notion of the manager as coach is firmly rooted in many of the larger organisations, in some of which you will not get promoted unless you can demonstrate an ability to coach. However, this coming into vogue has brought with it a number of issues that could undermine and discredit what is after all a very natural – maybe even instinctive – and human activity: to help others learn.

One issue is the appearance of executive coaches and life coaches, some of whom are not qualified for the job. In some parts of the USA, where half of all tarot-card readers have added the words 'executive coach' to their business card, the erosion of the credibility of coaching has already begun. Another issue, more relevant to this book, is the assumption that a two-day 'sheep-dip' style training programme will be sufficient to equip managers to go forth and coach. It takes more than that to learn to coach effectively. Such a programme may give a manager some skill but the real difficulty lies in applying the skill and in changing the relationship with those he manages. Few programmes offer sufficient support here and, because little of what is learned is put into practice, the coaching programme gets to be seen as flavour of the month – last month. Beyond these difficulties lie other issues, for instance there are many models of coaching but little agreement about what it is and about what a manager who coaches might look like.

In this book I hope to begin the process of defining effective coaching in work and to describe what a manager who coaches might look like. I say 'begin the process', because while I have quite some experience and some good ideas there is still a lot to be learned and I know, from sometimes embarrassing experience, that I do not have all the answers. I have written this book on the basis of what I know now. This implies that I have more to learn and that some aspects of the book, some definitions and distinctions, may not hit the spot. I hope this does not get in the way of your learning.

Chapter 1
The case for coaching

Coaching is now firmly on the agenda. The evidence is every-where: October 1998 saw the first-ever conference on coaching and mentoring in Europe; an article appears on almost a weekly basis in the business press; and most large organisations are either consid-ering implementing training for their management population or are already doing so. Executive coaching is a growth sector within consultancy.

Many people are now accustomed to constant change; indeed, some thrive on it. Whatever we might think about it – love it or fear it – change is here to stay. It is not that change was not there in the past; it was. It is just that the pace of change in work has accelerated, and it continues to accelerate. Market conditions, stock markets, innovation and development, and changing com-pany structures and roles all impact our actions on a daily basis. And these effects are felt despite a deep desire in many for a secure and recognisable status quo.

The most obvious response to these and other pressures has been to re-engineer the structures and systems that support our organi-sations. Yes, culture-change programmes have also been attemp-ted, but most of them have achieved only marginal success. The problem is that most of the culture-change programmes have been created from more or less the same mindset as the re-engineering programmes. But you cannot re-engineer people, even though many have tried to do so and others continue to try. 'Command and control' is a flight-path to extinction and 'engineering' is a manifestation of that mindset.

The pressures we are faced with – and I identify some of them below – demand increases in personal performance. That means people doing things differently, in creativity and above all in learning. In order to achieve change in these domains, we have to bring to bear a far greater understanding of how and why people do what they do, how and why they learn, and what inspires them. This can only be done through conversation, not least because the answers will be different for each individual.

So the way in which we relate to each other in the workplace must change. The way in which we talk to each other must change. This new way of relating (when I say 'new' I mean different from the current way, the traditional way) and these new ways of communicating are to a large part embraced by the notion of 'coaching'. Coaching by definition encourages learning, invites creativity and delivers higher performance. It respects the individual, builds confidence and generates a culture where responsibility sits with the performer, not the manager. In this way, people become accustomed to taking decisions and acting quickly and with flexibility.

➡ WORKING WITH CONSTANT CHANGE

Some of the pressures for change that can be encountered in the business world are set out below.

Fiercer competition

For most providers of product or services, it is a buyer market. Competition is fierce and any point of differentiation is immediately copied by those who would have your clients. There is hardly an organisation in the land that does not have its own version of 'you're only as good as your last deal'. And as more and more of the barriers to trade fall, either through political processes or increased access to high-speed telecommunications, competition will continue to get hotter.

Organisational re-structuring

The search for fitter organisations has unleashed wave after wave of reorganisation of the structure around which today's organisations have been built. Layers of management have been stripped out, collapsing the hierarchies and leaving managers with more people to manage and workers with more work to do.

Matrix management has meant that employees often have more than one person to whom they report. More and more of the actual work sits just outside the boundaries of 'my job', resulting in a workplace riven with project teams that meet to achieve a specific task and then disband.

The manager no longer the expert

One of the consequences of these restructurings is that managers often have people reporting to them who are more expert or knowledgeable in their job than the manager is. Supervision of a task is no longer possible, but support and guidance of the people doing the task is still required.

Customer expectations

Customers have become more demanding. Their expectations of service in terms of quality and speed have not only changed but continue to change. It seems that as purchasers we do not just want good customer service but a service that improves each time we use it. What was a great innovation in customer service yesterday becomes what I expect today as a matter of course; and I am now waiting expectantly for the next improvement, and if I do not get it I am unimpressed.

Furthermore, many organisations that are dependent on excellent customer relations are beginning to realise that front-line staff will only treat customers with respect if they in turn are treated with respect.

Workforce expectations

There is a new generation in the workforce nowadays, people who for the most part have no experience of hard times, such as the years during and immediately after the Second World War, and who are used to getting what they want. They are better educated, more sure of their rights as human beings, and more assertive; they have little or no respect for hierarchy. This group of people will not subordinate themselves to a manager; they will demand to be heard, will question and will not be bullied. For the most part, that is a very good thing.

➡ FULFILLING POTENTIAL: A NEW POSSIBILITY

Clearly, in order to stay abreast and competitive and ensure that employees can be sufficiently responsive, those managing need to adopt a different approach and relationship with those they manage.

There is, I think, more to this than just altering the way you as a manager interact with your staff. Positive interaction will produce some change, of course; but a far more fundamental shift is required in order that each member of your staff fufils his or her potential. That fundamental shift starts with you as manager. Your beliefs, values and expectations are a significant part of what creates the environment in which people either thrive or shrivel up. One important part of your role as a manager – and one that is a direct expression of your beliefs, values and expectations – is your ability to coach.

An example: coaching is not teaching

Example 1 is a description of a demonstration that a colleague gave at a workshop on coaching skills. It shows quite clearly what happens when the coach has gone through such a fundamental shift and is truly committed to the coachee's learning and does not get in the way of that learning process with instructions, advice or suggestions. Interestingly, this approach is not reliant on the coach being an expert in the topic of the session; in fact, there is not one technical instruction or suggestion in the whole session.

The topic for the session is 'how to improve catching' – in this case catching a ball. It requires a willing volunteer from the group, who believes that he cannot catch.

Example 1: Learning to catch

The coach positioned himself about twelve feet away from the volunteer and addressed him: 'To start with let's just see if you can catch at all. OK?' The volunteer, Peter, nodded but did not say anything. The coach threw a ball to him. Peter held out both his hands stiffly in front of him and his face screwed up with fear and anticipation. The ball passed just over the top of his hands, thumped into his chest and fell to the floor. Becoming embarrassed Peter grew even more tense.

The coach threw another ball. Peter reached out as before and missed completely. The coach threw another with the same result.

'Is that what you would expect?' the coach asked.

'Absolutely,' Peter replied in a small voice. 'I told you I couldn't catch and never could. Teachers in school would put me in goal just to get a laugh.'

'Is that what you're thinking when I throw the ball?'

'That, and . . . and all these people watching.'

The coach looked around at the people, some of whom had stood up and now formed a loose circle around them. 'Ah, don't worry about us' came a kindly voice.

The coach paused and caught Peter's attention. 'Tell me, Peter,' he said. 'If your catching was to get better, how would we know?'

PETER: 'Well I'd catch them, wouldn't I?'

COACH: 'All of them?'

PETER: 'Some of them.'

COACH: 'How many out of ten?'

PETER: 'Would you throw them in the exact same way as before?' he inquired suspiciously. The coach nodded. 'Then to catch one out of ten would be amazing.'

COACH: 'I know, but what would give you a sense of achievement?'

PETER: 'I'll say three out of ten.'

COACH: 'Great. Stay with me – I'm going to throw you some more balls. What I want you to do is watch the ball when it's in flight and, when you've caught it or whatever, tell me what you noticed about it. OK?'

PETER: 'So I'm to tell you what I notice about the ball when it's flying towards me?'

COACH: 'Exactly.'

The coach threw a ball. It brushed Peter's fingers as it went by him. 'What did you notice about the ball?'

PETER: 'Nothing.'

COACH: 'OK. Tell me what you notice about this one.' Again he threw a ball. Again Peter failed to catch it.

PETER: 'It's just yellow, greeney-yellow.'

Peter's response drew a snigger from the crowd. The coach, without taking his eyes from Peter, put a finger across his lips and the laughter stopped.

COACH: 'Fine. Tell me what you notice this time,' and he threw another.

PETER: 'It's got some writing on it,' said Peter as the ball bounced out of the palm of his hand.

COACH: 'Fine, so you've noticed the colour and the writing. Which is most interesting?'

PETER: 'The writing.'

COACH: 'OK. Tell me some more about the writing.' Again he threw another ball.

PETER: 'The writing is spinning. The ball is spinning,' Peter said as he caught the ball. There was a sharp intake of breath from behind. The coach did not respond.

COACH: 'Shall we stay with the spin?' he asked. Peter nodded. 'Tell me what you notice about the spin.' And once more he threw a ball.

PETER: 'It's spinning towards me, quite fast,' Peter said as he caught it again.

COACH: 'You've noticed both the direction of the spin and the speed of the spin. Which is most interesting?'

Peter paused. He threw the ball back to the coach.

PETER: 'Er . . . the direction.'

COACH: 'OK. Tell me which way this one is spinning,' the coach asked and then threw a ball. Peter reached out towards the ball and gracefully caught it, pulling his hands back towards himself in the act of catching, like a confident cricket player. He was completely relaxed, focused.

PETER: 'The top is spinning towards me and a little to the side.'

COACH: 'Which side?'

PETER: 'This way,' Peter said and described the direction of his finger in the air.

COACH: 'And this one?' the coach asked as he threw another.

PETER: 'Spinning the other way.'

COACH: 'And this one?' This one Peter completely failed to catch. 'What did you notice that time?'

PETER: 'Nothing at all.'

COACH: 'So where was your attention?'

Peter's face creased into a big grin.

PETER: 'I was thinking that I was catching a ball for the first time in my life. It's incredible!' He started laughing. The crowd clapped and laughed with him. 'How did you do that for me?'

COACH: 'We'll come back to that. Tell me how you did in relation to our goal of catching three out of ten?'

PETER: 'I've no idea. I must have caught three, though.'

One of the other participants in the workshop observed: 'You caught five out of eight by my counting.'

PETER: 'Wow. That many?'

COACH: 'Peter, are you willing to stop the exercise?'

PETER: 'Oh, just one more. Go on, it's fine.'

The coach turned to the participant who had made the observation. 'What did you notice about the exercise?'

The participant thought for a second. 'Mostly that you didn't tell him how to catch. You gave him no technical instruction.'

COACH: 'Anything else?'

Someone else added, 'What I noticed was how you got Peter to concentrate.'

COACH: 'How did I do that?'

There was a pause. One of the group responded: 'I remember. You just asked him what he noticed. And then . . .'

Here Peter joined in.

PETER: 'I noticed the colour and the writing . . . and you asked me to choose one . . . and I chose the writing.'

COACH: 'Yes. And then?' Nobody seemed to remember, so the coach filled in the blank. 'I think I asked you to tell me what you noticed about the writing.'

PETER: 'That's right. That's when I noticed that it was spinning,' Peter answered.

'I see what you were doing,' another participant chipped in. 'Each time Peter looked at the ball he noticed something more, some more detail, so after a while he was concentrating completely on the ball coming towards him.'

PETER: 'Yes,' Peter added, 'and the more I concentrated, the less I noticed the other people and I kind of forgot that I couldn't catch.'

Then another voice from the group asked: 'But how did he learn how to catch?'

COACH: 'To a degree he already knew,' the coach explained. Peter's seen others doing it and has tried before. So he had some information already. But, more importantly, with each attempt he learned something more – unconsciously. Peter always had the potential to learn how to catch; it's just that self-doubt and fear were getting in the way of the learning. When he got really focused, his natural ability to catch came to the fore. And I'll bet that if I had tried to teach in the more traditional way and given instructions, he would have got more tense and fearful and would have failed yet again.

COACH: 'Peter,' the coach said, 'thank you.'

Peter, smiling broadly, took a bow.

What the example illustrates

It is difficult to communicate on paper just how extraordinary the exercise described above is. Most people who witness it are completely taken by surprise. They have never seen such a dramatic shift in performance. They have never seen someone learn so quickly. They have seldom seen so much joy in so simple an exercise. Having seen the exercise most people want to know what happened and what the coach did.

The realisation that the coach did very little and that there was no technical instruction involved is the second surprise of the day. In a sense the paradigm that most people operate from, which tells them about how people learn and how quickly they can learn, has been blown apart. For some, this experience can be really uncomfortable and they will not believe the evidence of their eyes; some will not believe even after they have seen video playback of the exercise.

The best way to look at it is to suggest to you that coaching is about two words:

Potential   Performance

I have put these words on the page with a big gap between them because there is always a gap between performance and potential. And it is a huge gap. Even in the most ordinary activity, no matter how good someone is, they can always do better. However, there is something missing from the gap, and understanding this can help bridge it.

In the exercise just described, Peter had the ability to catch the ball, or at least the potential to learn very quickly how to do it. But something was getting in the way of this potential. Three of the things that were getting in the way of his potential were a false belief that he could not catch, a fear of looking stupid in front of the others in the group, and a confused or distracted state of mind. These are known as interference.

So the model becomes:

Potential minus interference
is equal to Performance

If you are a mathematician, you will have already worked out that in this equation the way to increase performance is to reduce the interference. As the interference gets less, more of the potential is available. One of the ways to reduce interference is to focus attention. When the attention is focused, the coachee enters a mental state in which learning and performance can be heightened.

➡ THE BASIC MODEL

This model comes from one of the most influential books on learning and performance of the last thirty years. It was written by Timothy Gallwey and is called *The Inner Game of Tennis* (Jonathan Cape, 1975). It caused a huge stir when it was published, and the ideas in it have been embraced by many thousands of people all over the world; it is still in print twenty-five years later. Gallwey called that mental state 'relaxed concentration'.

Most people that I ask have had an experience of this mental state, also called 'flow'. For some it has been a profound and moving experience, very often when engaged in a physical activity. A friend of mine used to race motor bikes and, occasionally, when he was absolutely on the limit, with his attention glued on the rider in front of him, he would get into flow. His thoughts and actions would become one, time would seem to slow down and the noise of the engines appeared to diminish. In this state he would sense exactly when the rider in front was going to make a tiny mistake and capitalise on it without hesitation.

But being 'in flow' does not have to be quite so dramatic. It can occur in such mundane activities as report writing. You sit down at your desk and get started. You make a number of false starts; your attempts are just not quite right. You get up, close the door, sit down and start again. And, suddenly, the words begin to come and you get into 'flow'. You look at your watch, an hour has gone by and you did not even notice it. And the report is half-written.

Before we move on, I suggest to you that the value of any time management system should be that it allows you to spend more time in 'flow'. It allows you to reduce interference so you can focus completely on the task at hand. You do not have to worry about other tasks because you have planned for them.

In this model a key part of the manager–coach's role is to help reduce the interference in the people he works with. This would be a remarkable shift of focus. Interference crops up in many forms. Here is a partial list that you might find familiar:

- fear (of losing, or winning, or of making a fool of yourself)
- lack of self confidence
- trying too hard

- trying for perfection
- trying to impress
- anger and frustration
- boredom
- a busy mind.

You can look at coaching in a number of ways, all of which are valid. You can look at it as a pragmatic way of interacting with colleagues at work to achieve higher performance. You can look at it as a route to releasing the potential of others. Or you can look at it as a philosophy that informs the way you live your life and the way you relate to others. None of these excludes any of the others. The point that I am trying to make is that coaching may be more than the next training programme that your organisation is going to send everyone on.

➡ THE CHARACTERISTICS OF A MANAGER–COACH

One of the things that inhibits managers from doing more coaching is that most of us do not have a good picture of what a manager who coaches might look like. I have often heard managers, who have been through a coaching-skills development programme and have come out with a degree of skill, say that they find it hard to know where to start. There is no doubt an element of excuse to this, but I have now heard it so often that I can only believe it to be true. I have some thoughts about the matter but suggest that you tackle the Exercise 1.1 first.

Exercise 1.1: A manager who coaches

Purpose: To develop a picture of what a manager who coaches might do and how he might be

Process

1 Identify a manager who has inspired you to greater effort. If you cannot think of one, identify a teacher or lecturer instead. Write down what it was about that person that inspired you.

2 What are the kinds of things he or she might do and the behaviours he or she might exhibit?

3 In your opinion, what key beliefs and values would a manager who coaches have? Write a list.

4 How do you imagine a manager–coach would relate to those he or she manages? List the characteristics.

Great coaches in the workplace are still too few, but the following characteristics are some of the hallmarks of such a person.

- *Great coaches believe in human potential* Coaches treat you with the respect you deserve as a fully functioning human being capable of many and great things. They respect your intelligence, creativity and intuition. Their expectation of you is that you will succeed and their belief in your capability probably exceeds your own. Should you fail in a task, their belief in you will not falter; they do not judge you.

- *Great coaches focus on learning* Organisations require results in order to survive. However, great coaches are more concerned for your learning than for your results. Very few people are in positions in which one mistake can cause the demise of the organisation, but if the vast majority of the staff stop learning then the organisation will surely collapse.

- *Great coaches let the coachees do the work* Coaches are interested in your good ideas and creativity and in your solutions to your problems. They do not dump their good ideas and solutions on you; rather, their listening and questioning allows you to explore a topic and make your own mind up, and then to progress in your own way. They leave responsibility with you.

- *Great coaches listen* Coaches listen to you because they believe in your potential. They know that you are a unique human being with a unique contribution to make and that, in order to understand what that contribution might be, they need to understand you.

- *Great coaches use the performance management system as a support* The annual appraisal occurs for many as a threat. Great coaches use the system to ensure that you have clarity in your role, know how you are doing and where you are going. In short, they ensure that you are focused and in 'relaxed concentration' as much of the time as possible. They understand that in order for you to give your best performance you need to be fulfilled and that there must be meaning to your work.

You may have noticed that I have not used the word 'empower' in this description. I hate the word. It seems to me that human beings are powerful in their own right. For someone to be empowered implies that the power has previously been removed. That business organisations and educational institutions do this as a matter of course is terrifying. Great coaches do not empower people; they know people have power and potential, and their job is to facilitate the expression of it.

Chapter 2
A definition of coaching

There is no commonly held definition of coaching. In order to understand what it is, most people refer to previous experience and often end up thinking of sports coaching. This is a useful analogy in some specific ways but is essentially quite different, the difference lying in the fact that most sports coaches operate from the belief that their job is, as an expert, to impart knowledge to the coachee. This seems to me to negate the way people actually learn – something I'll say more about later in this book. Others think of the extra maths coaching they had when they were failing at school and therefore have a negative impression of coaching: it is remedial.

Before we get to a better definition, I suggest that you try self-coaching Exercise 2.1.

Exercise 2.1: **The elements of effective coaching**

Purpose: To identify the elements of effective coaching.

Process

1 Identify a real situation where the intention was that you should learn something with the help of another. Choose a situation that was ineffective, i.e. you did not learn. The situation could be one encountered at work, in sport, at school or at university. Make a list of the specific elements of that situation that contributed to it being ineffective.

2 Identify a similar but effective situation, and make a list of the specific elements that contributed to it being effective.

3 From both lists choose the ten elements that, in your view at this point, are fundamental to effective coaching. Rate yourself on a scale of 1 to 10 against each of the elements.

4 Now write down what you need to learn in order to become a more effective coach.

➡ A TYPICAL DEFINITION

A commonly used definition of coaching is:

> *Coaching is the art of facilitating the performance, learning and development of another.*

It is worth looking at some of the individual words in this definition, and I choose to start with the word *performance*. Coaching in business is ultimately concerned with performance, and any intervention a coach might make should be driven by the intention to improve performance. Improved performance may relate to the execution of a specific task or project, the achievement of business goals or, more generically, greater effectiveness or efficiency.

Learning is another potential outcome from coaching and is at least as important as performance because, taking a longer-term view, it is what the future performance of the organisation is dependent upon. The distinction I would make with *development* is that while you have to learn in order to develop, 'learning' as used here refers to a broad domain – for example, how to approach a task or how to get to grips with new technology – while 'development' is about personal growth and greater self-awareness.

Then I come to *facilitating*. Here it means more than 'to make easy', although that is desirable too. 'Facilitating' implies that the person being coached has the capacity to think something through for themselves, to have an insight or some creative ideas. This in turn means that the coach has to give up on the assumption of having the right answer. The role of the coach is rather to enable the coachee to explore, to gain a better understanding, to become more aware and from that place to make a better decision than they would have made anyway.

Which leaves *art*. I do not mean to suggest that there is no science to coaching, for there is. Coaching is an art in the sense that, when practised with excellence, there is no attention on the technique but instead the coach is fully engaged with the coachee and the process of coaching becomes a dance between two people, conversationally moving in harmony and partnership. At this point the intelligence, intuition and imagination of the coach become a valuable contribution rather than an interference for the coachee.

The science to coaching comes out of experience and observation shared with like-minded people over a number of years and supported by other related disciplines such as psychology or philosophy. Much of this book is devoted to a description of that science, but you should know that the science of coaching is not the same as coaching. If you get stuck in doing it by the book, you are truly stuck; for you attention is with the book or the right way of doing it and not with the coachee. Someone once said of acting: 'There are no rules, but you've got to know them,' and coaching is a bit like that.

The context of the workplace

Before we move on I want to remind you that this book is about coaching in the workplace, and that context makes it different from coaching a friend, your offspring or a sports student. Work puts in place a number of constraints that in effect limit the scope of the conversation.

The coachee has almost certainly got a specific role and a number of objectives and commitments that he is bound to. In addition the organisation in which the coachee works will have a number of rules, implicit and explicit, that guide behaviour. In joining the organisation the coachee has chosen either to abide by these rules or change them by agreement.

The coach, and the coachee, has a responsibility to ensure that any actions that arise are consistent with the needs of the organisation. If they are not, and the coachee does not want to adapt, then it calls the coachee's place in the organisation into question. Such a discovery should not occur as a threat, because if the needs of the individual and the organisation are not congruent then neither party is happy and ultimately they should part company. Better that this be realised in a coaching session than a disciplinary meeting, so that it can be handled in a supportive and caring manner.

➡ THE SPECTRUM OF COACHING SKILLS

Coaching involves a relationship between people, and the conversation that takes place within that relationship can take a number of forms depending on the situation and the needs of the coachee. Figure 2.1 lays out most of the different conversational approaches a coach might take during a coaching session in the workplace.

An important distinction

I want to refer you to perhaps the most important distinction made in Figure 2.1, namely that between directive and non-directive coaching. This builds on the observations about facilitation that I made in Chapter 1.

'Directive coaching' means just that: to direct, to tell, to instruct coachees. It is the form of education and management that we are most familiar with, and which we pick up in our earliest days of schooling. Teacher knows and, like it or not, will tell you; you, on the other hand, sit there passively. The assumption is that once you have been told, you will know. And if you did not get it the first time, teacher merely has to increase the decibel level (because everyone knows that there is a direct correlation between understanding and speaking volume).

There is, however, an in-built limitation in the directive approach, which is that the coach has to know the answer or be able to work it out. Given the structures in most business organisations, where there are so many people reporting to a manager with different specialisms and unique issues, that is an unrealistic proposition. Surprisingly, the fact that a coach or manager does not know the answer does not seem to stop some of us.

Occasionally, as part of a training programme to develop coaching skills, I take the participants onto the tennis court. The purpose in this is to get them to deepen their *non*-directive

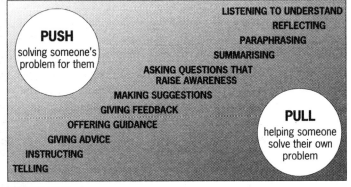

Figure 2.1: The Spectrum of Coaching Skills

coaching skills, the theory being that if they do not know the techniques involved in playing tennis they cannot resort to instructions. What baffles me is that participants who have never played tennis before will still try to tell their coachee how to play. It seems that the directive modelling of those early years is very powerful; people are trapped in 'teaching' and do not see that teaching has little to do with learning. What is amazing – and it amazes me every time I see it – is the results these coaches achieve when they adopt a non-directive approach. People learn in minutes things that would take a coach, operating from a more conventional model, hours to teach.

'Non-directive coaching' is, again, just that: you do not direct, instruct or tell. To illustrate what I mean, let me remind you how you learned to walk. You learned to walk through direct experience, a kind of trial and error. You stood up and had a go; you fell over; and, unconsciously, your body–mind processed the information gained from your experience so as to make the appropriate corrections. I bet that 90% of you are still walking well today and that you have never had any instructions in how to do it.

Let me also tell you what did *not* happen when you learned to walk. A willing parent did not stand behind you, armed with *The Book That Has Been Handed Down Through The Ages*, in order to issue you with a series of instructions: 'Good boy. Now put all your weight on your right leg. OK. Let your left leg swing forward. Try to get some balance with your arms. No, stupid, your *left* leg! . . .' You get the picture. Nor were there recriminations, punishments and blame when you got it wrong: parents in the early days are blessed with a non-judgemental approach that encourages experimentation and playfulness. But then somewhere along the line we, as parents/teachers/managers, forget this lesson. Each one of us is born with an innate capacity to learn, a sort of learning instinct if you will. A non-directive coach seeks to tap into that instinct so that the coachee learns for herself or himself.

Despite my passionate insistence about the limitations of a directive or 'tell' approach, it is important to understand that the 'directive' end of the spectrum is available to you as a coach too. There will be times when you know the answer and the coachee is stuck; and there will be times when your coachee needs some feedback or advice. In these situations, to withhold an answer or some feedback or advice would not be helpful. In Chapters 4 and 5 we will look in more depth at the skill set of an effective coach, exploring the full spectrum shown in Figure 2.1.

➡ LEADERSHIP, MANAGEMENT AND COACHING

It would be a great disservice to you and the notion of coaching if we did not relate it to the other aspect of a manager's job. If a manager sees his role solely in terms of coaching, then he will probably fail to exactly the same degree that traditional managers are currently failing who do not recognise coaching. (This is true of organisations that have a hierarchical structure in which authority and power is invested in the manager. There are a few organisations experimenting with structures that encourage coaching relationships in which this assertion may not be true.)

Figure 2.2 shows three overlapping domains, namely the domains of leadership, management and coaching. Each of these domains has distinct and different requirements, and a manager needs to fulfil all of these in order to deliver to the organisation the best performance of his staff.

In the domain of leadership, the requirement is to create and maintain a vision – a picture of the future – and to deliver that future by making sure it is accounted for in peoples actions in the present. In the domain of management, the requirement is to deliver results within pre-agreed parameters. These parameters are the vision and goals of the organisation, the desired culture and behaviours, the management systems, and the promises to share-holders and customers. In the domain of coaching, the requirement is to ensure the learning and development of the people with whom there is a line-management relationship.

The domains overlap because there are some requirements that fall into more than one domain. For instance, the leadership domain and the management domain overlap when there is a need to ensure that whatever vision or goals are agreed in, say, the managers team are congruent with the vision that the organisation as a whole is pursuing. Coaching and management domains overlap when a manager, in conducting an appraisal, uses coaching to establish what the staff member's goals are.

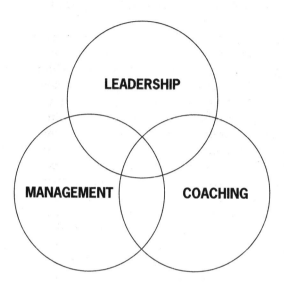

Figure 2.2: Leadership, management and coaching

The domains also overlap because, if they are viewed from the perspective of the skills employed to deliver on the requirement, the skills particular to one domain sometimes find appropriate application in another. For instance, in leadership mode, I may choose to use a coaching style or a facilitative style to create a vision that all the team are bought into. Or I may use a coaching approach to help someone identify their personal values so that they can appreciate how their values relate to the corporate values.

Problems arise when the manager is not clear which domain he is in, because the rules in each of the domains are different. In coaching, the coachee can expect that anything he says will be treated with complete confidence, whereas in a management situation the same confidentiality will almost certainly not exist – the manager may need to inform others of issues or outcomes. A good coach makes sure that both parties know which domain they are in, and discusses the ground rules relevant to that domain.

Management and coaching are in some ways incompatible. Coaching requires a relationship of great trust, where it is safe for the coachee to be vulnerable, safe to acknowledge weaknesses and mistakes, and safe to simply not know something. It is only in such an environment that learning can happen, that a coachee can test out new ideas. If the coach is also the manager, it may be difficult – or simply unwise – to own up to a weakness because that manager has significant control over a staff member's rate of pay and career prospects. It is not that it is an impossible situation; it is just so that managers have significant power within the relationship and many have a propensity to use it. Coaching can only happen in a management relationship if there is trust. If there is no trust, do not bother coaching; instead, build the relationship.

➡ **MENTORING, COUNSELLING AND COACHING**

Mentoring and coaching

I suggested earlier in this chapter that, in relation to coaching, there is not a huge amount of agreement about what exactly it is. This makes it difficult to differentiate mentoring from coaching. But let me have a go.

A mentor is someone – usually more senior or more experienced – who is appointed or chosen to help and advise another employee. The relationship is almost always outside any line-management relationship. The objectives are usually long term and centre around the mentee's progress in his career.

A coach is someone who is chosen (never appointed) and often from outside the organisation or from outside the line-management arrangements. The objectives of the relationship relate primarily to the achievement of business goals. I say that the coach is never appointed, meaning that a coachee must always have the right to choose their coach for the coaching to work. A coachee will not be open and relaxed with a coach whom they do not trust or with whom they cannot build a relationship.

Where the coach is also the manager (see previous section) there needs to be great clarity concerning which of the domains of leadership, management or coaching apply and the relevant ground rules.

Counselling and coaching

The core skills involved in counselling and coaching, and even mentoring, are very similar, if not actually the same. These are principally the skills of listening and of asking questions. They are the skills towards the non-directive end of the spectrum of coaching skills (see Figure 2.1).

For this reason, coaching and counselling are difficult to differentiate. However it is important to distinguish between the two as a coach is seldom qualified to operate in the domain of a counsellor or therapist and to do so is potentially dangerous.

I make a distinction between coaching and counselling that works for me. I have got to hold up my hand and acknowledge that many counsellors do not like the distinction I make here, but for all that it has a certain validity.

Counselling is concerned with the individual and with the relationship between the individual and the context in which that individual operates, both family and community (see Figure 2.3). Since most counselling is remedial, the intent is to help the individual become 'whole' and to find their place within their family and community.

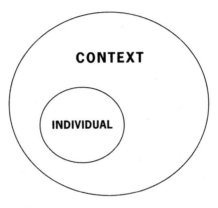

Figure 2.3: Individual and context

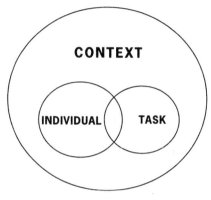

Figure 2.4: Individual, task and context

Coaching differs somewhat because it also takes into consideration the task or work that the individual is engaged in. As shown in Figure 2.4, coaching is concerned with:

- the individual
- the relationship between the individual and their task or job
- the context of the organisation in which the individual works.

The context also includes the individual's family and community, although, typically, these only become a matter for discussion if they are inhibiting performance of the task.

This analysis gives us one guideline as to what appropriate content for a coaching session might be. A topic gets on the coaching agenda if it relates to the successful execution of the task. So if the coachee wants to talk about the squash match they had the night before with their best friend where the best friend cheated, this is probably not an appropriate topic for a coaching session – at least not one on company time.

It is probably impossible to create a complete distinction between coaching and counselling. I know that as a coach I have had appropriate conversations with coachees that a counsellor could have handled just as well. What is important is not so much the distinction between the two but to know, as a coach, when you are out of your depth, i.e. when the skill and understanding that you possess are not sufficient to support the coachee.

Fortunately there are some checks and balances:

- A coachee typically only reveals what they feel safe in revealing. Most coachees have an intuitive sense of what is appropriate and of the skill and experience of the coach and do not cross that boundary.

- The coach equally has an intuitive sense of what is appropriate and what he or she is capable of dealing with.

- A well set-up coaching programme will have a clear set of goals. If the coach is concerned that the topic for a session is not appropriate, then it serves both parties to ask how discussing it relates to achieving the goals of the programme. This helps the coachee to stand back and re-assess the situation.

It is likely at some point in your life as a coach that you will find yourself out of your depth, maybe where the conversation has a strong emotional content and the coachee is in distress. The appropriate thing to do at this point is to stop coaching, to say explicitly that you want to end the coaching session, and that you want to end it because you are out of your depth. Ask the coachee how they want to take the matter forward and, if possible, guide them towards counselling or therapy. Be really clear that to stop coaching does not mean that you stop listening. You need to stay with the coachee until they have regained sufficient composure to take the next step.

➡ EFFECTIVE COACHING

This part of the book has been an attempt to define coaching, to give it its proper place in the workplace and to distinguish it from other similar activities. The shortcoming here is that we are only looking at one model of coaching. There are many coaches working who employ other models and other approaches.

The most common coach is the sports coach and almost universally the model they employ is 'coach as expert'. Some of them are very successful. However, their ability to teach is limited to what they know. This works in sport, to a degree, because a coach can know a significant chunk of what there is to know about a particular discipline. This model does not transfer to the business environment very well for all the reasons described earlier in Chapter 1.

In the world of work, you may also came across coaches whose approach is based on a particular psychology or philosophy. Two approaches that have particular prominence are Neuro Linguistic Programming (NLP) and Transformational Technology. These are extremely useful, but neither of them is coaching in and of itself although they can inform coaching and provide some powerful tools.

The non-directive approach to coaching, as described earlier in this chapter, has proved to be the most effective in the workplace. Most if not all the leading experts promulgate an approach similar to this. I have called this book *Effective Coaching,* and 'effective' in this context means a number of things:

- *Extraordinary business results.* Without any intervention at all, most people will achieve average business results with maybe an incremental improvement over the previous year. Coaching should create a step-change in the results as the coachee becomes more focused and committed.

- *A focus on learning.* To achieve the business result is one thing; to achieve it in a way in which the coachee learns as part of the process has a greater value – to the coachee, the coach and the organisation.

- *Motivation is intrinsic to the process of coaching.* That the coach respects the coachee as well as the coachee's ideas and opinions, that the coachee is doing work in a chosen manner, that the coachee is pursuing goals and taking responsibility makes for a coachee who is enthusiastic and committed.

- *Responsibility stays with the coachee.* If a coach solves the problem or decides on the course of action for a coachee, then the coach has taken ownership of the issue. Should the coachee hit an obstacle, he or she will come back to the coach for more guidance. Effective coaching, where the coachee solves the problem or develops a plan to solve it, has the result that responsibility stays with the coachee.

If the above are the hallmarks of effective coaching, then the only approach that can achieve all of them is a non-directive approach.

Chapter 3
Managing a coaching session

This chapter tells you how to control a coaching session. As will be obvious by now, you cannot control the content of a session; that belongs to the coachee. However, to be effective as a coach you need to be in control of the things that you are in control of, namely yourself and the structure and process of the session. Being in control of oneself would be a good idea, to the degree that it is possible, and I touch on it in Chapters 10 and 11. Being in control of the structure and the process is an easier game.

Be clear too that you are only in control of the session by agreement with the coachee. At the extreme, this means that if the coachee does not agree, then there is no session. You need to remember too, however, that the coach also has rights and does not have to engage in the session if he or she feels that what the coachee is asking for cannot be delivered, whether for reasons of ethics or integrity or lack of experience or skill.

➡ THE GROW MODEL

The best model to help you structure a session is the GROW model. The practice of effective coaching was already in place before the GROW model was 'discovered'. Some bright soul, having observed a number of sessions saw a pattern in those sessions and said 'this is what you are doing' and the observed pattern was developed as the GROW model. I tell you this because, for many people, the first use of the model feels unnatural and I want you to know that once you have used it a few times it begins to feel fluent, to the point where you hardly have to think of it.

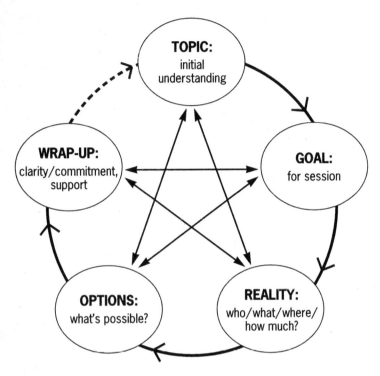

Figure 3.1: The GROW model

As can be seen from the diagram in Figure 3.1, the first letters of each of the stages in the model (working clockwise) give you GROW. Well, almost. What is missing is the first and rather critical stage, that of identifying the topic for the session. Attempts to include this stage in the mnemonic have, without exception, been clumsy – the best was the TO GROW model, borrowing the 'TO' from topic. In any case, that suggestion was too late because the model had already gained some currency.

If you imagine someone coming to you for some coaching, a sequence of questions might be posed to the coachee that go something like the following:

- 'What do you want to talk to me about?' (Topic)
- 'What's actually happening?' (Reality)
- 'What could you do about it?' (Options)
- 'What are you definitely going to do about it?' (Wrap-up)

The only missing element from this perspective of the model is the goal. I have not put it here, because in my experience it is neither a natural nor obvious question to ask, at least not initially. However, as I will show later in this chapter, establishing a goal for a session is vital for success. Let me take you through each of the stages of the model. For the sake of this exercise, we will assume that there is someone willing to be coached and that the preliminaries necessary in forming a contract have been dealt with (see Chapter 8). You, the coach, and your coachee are sitting comfortably, ready to begin.

Topic

This is the first stage in the session. It is not a detailed account of the subject-matter at this point. What you want to understand at this stage is what territory you are in, the scale of the topic, its importance to the coachee, and sometimes the emotional significance for the coachee (see Example 2). It is sometimes useful to establish what the coachee's longer-term vision or goal for the topic is.

The desired outcome for this stage is an initial understanding of what the coachee wants to talk about.

Example 2: Defining the topic

COACH: What would you like to talk about?

COACHEE: As you know, I've got to make a presentation to the Board next week and I'm a bit nervous about doing a good job.

COACH: Tell me some more about that.

COACHEE: The team has asked me to make the presentation on Project Blue and I am not at all sure how I should approach it.

COACH: Right.

COACHEE: And if I tell the truth I'm a bit nervous about standing up in front of the Board. They have a reputation for being tough on people who don't present well.

COACH: Yes, I know. Is there anything else about this that you'd like to discuss?

COACHEE: Not really – well, yes. The last time I made a presentation to a senior group, it didn't go very well.

COACH: Is there a broader issue here, then, about your presentation skills?

COACHEE: I guess so.

COACH: Specifically, then, what is the topic for the session?

COACHEE: It's about making a good presentation to the Board, and also about improving my presentation skills in general.

G for Goal

While all the stages of the model are critical, the Goal stage has perhaps the greatest impact on the success of the session. What you are looking to establish is a goal for the session, something that will be achieved within the confines of the discussion (see Example 3). This should not be a long-term vision or goal.

I have an image for this for myself. I have a tent on a beach – rather Victorian, like a Punch and Judy stall. Above the entrance is a sign that says, 'Your problems solved. $50 or your money back'.

When my client enters, we establish a contract in the form of an outcome for the session. I do not get paid unless that outcome is achieved. (Just so you know, the tent is somewhere warmer than the UK; otherwise the season would not be long enough to make a decent income!).

The desired outcome for the stage is a set of clear, specific and measurable outcomes.

Example 3: Defining the goal

COACH: OK. I think I've got a fair understanding of the topic for the session. Tell me what you would like to get out of this session?

COACHEE: Well, I'm more concerned about the immediate problem, the presentation to the Board than I am about reaching the longer term thing – being happy to speak to groups of fifty or more. So I'd like to focus more on the session with the Board.

COACH: Fine. And tell me what you want from this session.

COACHEE: Well, I'd like to understand what went wrong in the presentation to the senior managers that I mentioned, and I'd like to get an idea of the key things to do differently next week.

COACH: There are two parts to that: to understand what went wrong and to have an idea of the key things to do differently. Take the first bit. What outcome would you want from understanding what went wrong?

COACHEE: To have identified the key lessons.

COACH: What does 'key' mean?

COACHEE: The most important – the two or three things that make or break a presentation.

COACH: And for the second bit, the key things to do differently? What outcome would you like for that?

COACHEE: Obviously the discussion about what went wrong may give me some of the things to do differently, but I suspect there are some other things that I need to know.

COACH: And the outcome?

COACHEE: If I could find in the whole session five or six key things to do or remember for the Board presentation, that would be great.

R for Reality

The reality stage of the model is concerned with achieving the most accurate picture of the situation or the topic that can be achieved. It is a bit like placing all the pieces of a jigsaw puzzle face up on the table, noticing how the bits fit together and how the pattern forms. Out of all the jumble, a picture – improved understanding – emerges.

The role of the coach in this stage of the process, as in all others, is simply to understand. Just that. No wisdom, no good ideas, no jumping to conclusions. The desired outcome of the stage is the clearest possible understanding of the situation or topic (see Example 4).

Example 4: Establishing the reality

COACH:　You've mentioned the presentation that didn't work so well and then this other, more generic, 'other things you might do'. Are there any other elements to this?

COACHEE:　Not that I can think of.

COACH:　Which of the two do you want to tackle first?

COACHEE:　I think the obvious place to start is with the presentation that I messed up.

COACH:　OK. Tell me about that.

COACHEE:　It was in an earlier stage of this project and again it was my turn to present – we take it in turns. I thought it was going to be relatively straightforward but in the event it turned out all wrong.

COACH:　Just how bad was it?

COACHEE:　It wasn't a *complete* disaster, and they *did* get the message. It was that I really didn't do our project work, or myself, justice.

COACH:　So what actually happened?

COACHEE:　I was a bit flustered when I got there. We had worked late the night before and at that point I thought I knew what I had to do. However, on the morning I felt unprepared. I was still putting the slides in order minutes before I was due to start.

COACH:　What else happened?

COACHEE:　Apart from not feeling prepared, I was really nervous and my words came out a bit scrambled. At one point someone asked me to repeat what I had just said because they had not understood.

COACH: Was there anything else in the session that didn't work for you?

COACHEE: Yes. I was unsettled by a number of the questions. I don't think that anyone was trying to be difficult, but I just found it difficult to find the answers.

COACH: So far in this conversation you've mentioned something about your preparation, about feeling nervous, and the difficulty you had in answering questions. Is there anything else that you remember?

COACHEE: Not really. That's enough to work with.

COACH: Which of those three things would you like to focus on first?

COACHEE: The bit about handling questions. That was the worst bit.

O for Options

Once the clearest possible understanding of the situation or topic has been reached, the discussion naturally turns to what can be done, i.e. to what is possible for the coachee to do. I use 'possible' as in 'That's a possibility', namely in the biggest and most creative sense rather than in a narrow or restrictive one. The intent here is to draw out a list of all that is possible, without judgement or evaluation (see Example 5).

The desired outcome is the longest list of all that is possible for the coachee to do (in order to satisfy the session goal).

Example 5: Listing the options for action

COACH: We've spoken in some detail about preparation, nervousness, and handling questions. In looking to move forward, which of those would you like to pursue first?

COACHEE: I still think there is most mileage in the handling-questions bit. If I can get that right, it will help with the nervousness issue. And the preparation bit should be relatively easy to crack.

COACH: Where we got to with handling questions, as I understood you, was that you felt that you had not always fully understood the question you had been asked.

COACHEE: Yes, and that was partly because I was thinking of my next slide.

COACH: So what could you do differently?

COACHEE: I could make sure that no questions were asked till the end of the session.

COACH: What else?

COACHEE: I could just stop myself from going to the next slide – maybe make eye contact. That would help.

COACH: Anything else?

COACHEE: I'm not sure. Well, if I haven't heard properly, I could ask the questioner to repeat the question. Or if I think I've heard but I'm not sure, I suppose I could check my understanding by repeating the question.

W for Wrap-up

The final stage of the model is Wrap-up. Lots of options have been listed, and the remaining issue is to select the most appropriate and agree the next steps.

It is often useful to check the coachee's commitment to the chosen course of action and to see if any support is required. It is almost always useful to get the coachee to say exactly what their action plan is – some coaches have a tendency to say 'So your action plan is . . .' but if the coachee states the action plan it ensures clarity and agreement and, from the tone of their voice, the coach can ascertain the coachee's level of commitment (see Example 6).

The desired outcome from this stage is a commitment to action. Any actions that are agreed should be as specific as possible and in an agreed time-frame.

Example 6: Wrapping-up the coaching session

COACH: Of all the options that we have identified, which ones do you think you might action?

COACHEE: I can't remember them all.

COACH: I think I jotted down most of them. There are those options that came out of the discussion about the presentation, concerning preparation, nervousness and handling questions. Then there were the options that came out of the second part of the discussion. Where do you want to start?

COACHEE: Lets start with the handling questions bit.

COACH: You came up with four options: keeping the questions to the end of the session; stopping and making eye contact; asking the questioner to repeat the question; and playing your understanding of the question back.

COACHEE: That's right. The only one I'm uncomfortable about is the first one; keeping questions till the end.

COACH: What is it that makes you uncomfortable?

COACHEE: Despite the fact that I am not very good at it – yet – I do want to keep the sessions as interactive as possible. So I think I'll skip that one. The others I can do.

COACH: Just so we are both sure, tell me specifically what you are going to do.

COACHEE: In the presentation to the Board, when I hear a question I will stop thinking of what I have to do next and make eye contact with the questioner. If I don't hear the question fully, I will either ask the person to repeat it or, if I've got the gist of it, I will check my understanding by playing it back.

COACH: OK. Now which part do you want to tackle next?

. . .

The GROW Model is shown as a circle in Figure 3.1 because in the most straightforward sessions you move from Topic to Goal to Reality to Options to Wrap-up and then probably contract to a time and a place for the next session, when you move back to Topic.

The arrows between the stages reflect the fact that not all sessions are straightforward and that you may have to shuffle between the stages. For instance, in the Wrap-up the coachee may identify a new option or, in the Reality stage, it may become clear that the goal is in fact inappropriate. If this happens, simply return to the relevant part of the model. Do not get hung up on its linear nature – few coachees think in a linear fashion and your job is to follow their interest.

Chapter 4
The key skills of coaching

Chapter 3 outlines a structure to guide a coach through a session, and from reading the text in the Examples of the coaching stages you will have begun to detect some of the relevant skills.

This chapter looks at some of those skills in greater depth, in particular:

- listening
- raising awareness
- asking questions.

➡ **LISTENING**

In a relationship between you and me, the closest we can get to the experience of listening is your attending to the words on the page. And within the confines of this book, a blank page is the closest that I can get to silence. As you look at that blank page, it is my guess that your experience is not of blankness but rather of all the ideas that you can read into the space. In effect, you fill the page for me with your own thoughts – your ideas, opinions, expectations, conjecture, assumptions and judgements. And even as you read this page, your thoughts will spin off onto some flight of fancy, or something in your environment will distract you.

For most of us the experience of listening is very similar. Sometimes on a workshop I will give the participants a simple listening exercise to do. When the exercise is over, I will ask them what got in the way of their listening – what the interference was – and will note down their responses. This is a typical list:

- other people talking
- what I thought they were going to say
- what I thought they should say
- they were boring
- I had already worked out what they should do
- I had thought of what they were saying already
- what I was thinking was more interesting
- thinking of the next question
- thinking of my response
- what's for dinner
- why is he wearing that tie?

That little voice in the head is going wild, and it almost never stops. There is so much going on in our own minds that to make sufficient space for another person is difficult. At this point in the workshop, some participants get upset because they value their own thoughts and ideas, are entertained by their assumptions and revel in their judgements. That's fine – fine, of course, so long as they do not try to coach someone or pretend that they are listening.

In coaching, the purpose of listening is to understand – fully.

This is because when you really listen to another person – when you understand them to the best of your ability – something extraordinary happens: *the speaker (the coachee) typically arrives at a better understanding of the topic for themselves.* And out of that better understanding, that seeing of things more clearly, people make better choices.

Imagine a spring-loaded stack of plates such as you might find in a canteen. As you take the top plate the next one is pushed up. Each plate represents an idea or notion that rises into my consciousness. As a thought enters my consciousness and I pass it on to a listener, the next thought is pushed up. And I pass that one on. And then the next. Somewhere down in my stack of plates – in my set of ideas – is my solution, my creative idea, my insight. If someone is willing to listen to me, then I may get to that place, that plate, that thought. And because the thought is uniquely mine, I will nurture it, develop it and put it to some creative use.

On the other hand, if my coach takes the first few plates, assumes that he now understands and then gives me back my plates and a few of his own – his own good ideas, his way forward on my issue – I have not really learned anything and I do not own the outcome.

Techniques to improve listening

There are a number of things you can do to improve your listening. The first is simple, but not necessarily easy: start noticing when you are not listening. The second is a discipline called 'managing your communication cycles'. Thirdly, the repeating, summarising and paraphrasing of material can help. And, lastly, silence can be golden. Each of these techniques is described further below.

Start noticing you're not listening

It is important to realise when you are not properly listening. In those circumstances you must gently bring your attention back to the speaker. This has one major flaw as a tactic, in that the only time you become aware that you have 'gone away with your thoughts' is when you return – or when the speaker gives you some feedback, which may be too late. If this happens, the only thing to do that has any integrity to it is to own up. It is not likely the speaker will be surprised; they will have noticed, probably before you did.

Managing your communication cycles

I find this particularly useful when demonstrating coaching in public. The potential for distraction is so great and nerves so a-jangle that I need something quite overt to keep me focused.

Use the Communication Cycle shown in Figure 4.1 to help you manage conversations when there is a need for quality listening in order to understand. You do not need to do this for every conversation; indeed, if you did you would exhaust yourself and those around you.

A prerequisite for communication is a minimum of two people – in our context a coach and a coachee. The first part of the cycle is called 'initiation', where the coach asks a question or issues an instruction to the coachee. The second part is called the 'response', the coachee having understood the initiation answers. The response must be congruent with the initiation.

Example 7: Congruent and incongruent responses

COACH: Tell me how you got on with your action plan from our last session. [Initiation]

COACHEE: I had a truly miserable week. One of my clients pulled out of a deal at the last minute and . . . [Incongruent response]

COACH: Sorry, we can return to that if you want, but tell me how the action plan went.

COACHEE: Oh, the action plan. I got most of it done, I'd say ninety per cent. I couldn't complete writing up my career vision because I ran out of time. Not bad, considering the difficulties. [Congruent response]

However, the Cycle is not complete here. The Communication Cycle is only complete when the coachee knows that he or she has been understood. So the final part is called 'acknowledgement'. At the start of a session, and particularly with a new client, the acknowledgement will take the form of a full summary or paraphrasing of what has been said. This is because the coach

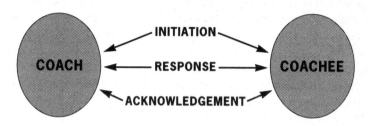

Figure 4.1: The Communication Cycle

needs to be absolutely certain that he has understood. It is also because the coachee needs reassuring that he has been understood.

Example 8 (continued from above): Acknowledgement

COACH: Let me confirm that I have understood. Despite some difficulties, you got ninety per cent of the action plan done. The bit you didn't quite finish was your career vision because you ran out of time. Is that right?

As the session progresses and trust develops in the relationship, the need to summarise or paraphrase diminishes. You will still need to manage your Communication Cycles but now 'I understand', a grunt or a nod of the head signals the acknowledgement.

Another way to signal that you have understood is to ask a further question congruent with the response. In our example above, the coach might ask, 'Tell me about the difficulties.'

The cycle is then complete and a new one starts. This may seem like a tedious process to engage in. As with the GROW model, I would like you to know that for the most part it happens quite naturally and is typically unnoticed by the coachee. Their experience is of being completely understood, probably for the first time. From my own experience I know that, when engaging with a new client with a difficult issue, it is the discipline of managing each Communication Cycle that has generated real understanding and been the foundation of a successful coaching session.

Repeating, summarising and paraphrasing

Powerful aspects of listening in order to understand are repeating verbatim, summarising and paraphrasing of material that has been discussed.

Repeating verbatim gives a clear signal to the coachee that you have at least heard the words. But a tape recorder can do that, and what repetition does not do is signal that you have fully understood. It has its place in coaching when a particular set of words, or word, has significance for the coachee. That you have picked up on that significance is a demonstration of your understanding.

Summarising: presenting in shortened form or extracting the essence is another demonstration of your understanding. In coaching it is best used to check understanding, for example after the coachee has made a number of points or at the end of a stage of the GROW model. It is a bit like using the 'save' key on your computer; all that information is stored (understood) so the coachee can feel free to move on.

A good way to use these particular tools is to turn them around and have the coachee summarise or paraphrase. It can generate great clarity in what is truly important for the coachee. It is also a good trick if you have lost the thread and either don't have the courage to own up or deem it inappropriate: 'There was a lot there. Could you summarise it for me?'

Something special often happens here when the coach summarises or paraphrases: new insights or ideas often come to light for the coachee. I can only guess why that might happen. I think it is that, as the coachee hears the issues played back, it is possible to get a little distance from them – to be not so much attached – and in seeing them differently have some new thoughts. It is always easier to solve someone else's problem, when there really is distance.

The issue of distance is important in coaching. If a coachee is caught up in a difficult or emotional topic, there is no distance and this almost *creates* the problem. For instance, I remember sitting on the top deck of a red London bus travelling into the West End in heavy traffic. As the bus approached a junction I could see, before it actually happened, that we were heading for a complete logjam. Four cars at the junction had managed to get into positions from which none could easily move. From the top of the bus it was easy to see the solution. *If the blue car just pulled back a few feet that would allow the red car* . . . However, for the driver of the blue car it is a different matter. He gets angry and frustrated: 'Just what I need when I'm late. Where did that !****! in the red car come from? Shouldn't be allowed on the road. . . .' The driver of the blue car has become the problem. If he could only see it – the logjam and himself – from a better perspective, the problem could be solved. Get some distance.

Good coaching can help people gain some distance, be less involved and make some better choices. The driver of the blue car joins the coach in the top of the bus. The process of talking to the coach, of good reflecting back – either through summary or the gentle raising of an eyebrow – or of simply being understood can create that distance.

Using silence

Novice coaches are often afraid of silences in their coaching sessions and will jump in with more speech, perhaps another question. A lot of valuable reflection can be lost when this happens. Silence is truly golden in a coaching session. Typically, it means that the coachee is busy thinking or processing something internally. When they are ready to respond again, they will tell you.

There is, of course, another kind of silence, which occurs when the coachee does not know what he is supposed to be doing. In this case, move the session on. It is usually pretty easy to tell when someone is thinking something through and when they are not, so look for the visual signals, for instance being still, eyes focused on the middle distance are good signs that someone is engaged with their thoughts.

➡ RAISING AWARENESS

In coaching, the purpose of listening is to understand. In understanding the coachee, the coachee's awareness is raised and the coachee can make better choices.

The first time I opened the bonnet of a car I saw a mass of metal with pipes and hoses and wiring. Because I did not understand what I was seeing, I was powerless to fix the car or to improve its performance. As I began to understand the function of the various items and the relationships between them – as my awareness was raised – I became powerful (at least in the context of that particular engine) and could make the necessary repairs and improvements. So it is with coaching generally.

Let me describe to you (via Example 9) the impact of raised awareness in a learning situation – in this case a tennis lesson. This is familiar territory for me because it is where I started coaching and where I first discovered the magic of a non-directive approach. We will join the lesson some way into it when the topic and goal for the session have already been agreed. The coachee wants to improve a particular stroke, his forehand.

Example 9: Coaching at tennis

COACH: I am going to hit about six balls to your forehand. What I want you to do is to notice what's happening. Whatever stands out for you. OK?

[Coachee nods agreement and coach hits the balls to him, one at a time.]

COACH: What did you notice?

COACHEE: Well, the balls went all over the place and I felt really out-of-control.

COACH: Hit another few balls and then tell me which of those is most interesting.

[A few strokes later]

COACHEE: This out-of-control thing is the most interesting.

COACH: Hit some more and tell me more about it.

COACHEE: It just feels out-of-control.

COACH: All the time, throughout the stroke?

[More strokes]

COACHEE: No, mostly when the racket is back here. [Coachee indicates problem area]

COACH: Hit some more and tell me where exactly the problem occurs. Does it happen when you are taking the racket back, at the moment when it stops going back and starts coming forward, or when it's coming forward.

[Coachee hits some more balls. The shots were initially spraying the adjacent tennis courts and are now beginning to land in the court.]

COACHEE: Interesting. It happens just as the racket starts coming forward.

COACH: OK. Hit some more balls. This time after each stroke I want you to tell me how out-of-control it felt. Use a scale of one to ten. One is complete control and ten is completely out-of-control.

COACHEE: Eight . . . eight . . . nine . . . seven . . . seven . . . six . . . four . . . four . . . three.

[As the coachee gains control, the shots are becoming more and more accurate. The last four have all been over the net and within the court lines. He's beginning to relax and enjoy it.]

What is happening in this session is that the coachee's level of awareness about what he is actually doing is heightening with each stroke. The learning instinct that I referred to earlier has kicked in, and the body–mind is getting high-quality information that is allowing it to quickly make the necessary adjustments. In coaching, the purpose of any intervention – listening, asking questions, summarising or paraphrasing, giving feedback or making suggestions – is to raise awareness.

➡ ASKING QUESTIONS

Another way of deepening understanding, and thereby raising awareness, is to ask questions. There are a number of different types of questions that are effective in coaching, such as:

- questions that follow interest
- questions that clarify
- questions that tie things down.

These are explored further below.

Questions that follow interest

Just say, for a minute anyway, that people had potential – that they could really solve their own problems and be creative *all on their own* without any help from you or me. If that really were the case how would we listen to them and how would we ask questions? Questions that start with, 'Don't you think . . .' and 'Have you thought of . . .' would be redundant, because they are concerned with the coach's thinking ('I've got this good idea') rather than the coachee's thinking.

Asking questions that follow interest is one way of respecting the fact that the coachee can think for himself or herself. In Example 10, we have a condensed version of the ball-catching demonstration that I described in Chapter 1. Notice the use of questions that follow interest. In between each of the coach's question or instructions he throws a ball.

Example 10: Following interest

COACH: Tell me what you notice about the ball when it's in flight.

COACHEE: It's green.

COACH: Thank you. Tell me what you notice this time.

COACHEE: It's got some writing on it.

COACH: OK. Tell me what you notice this time.

COACHEE: The writing again.

COACH: OK. And see what you notice this time.

COACHEE: The lines on the ball.

COACH: Notice anything else?

COACHEE: No, just those things.

COACH: Which of the three things you've mentioned – the colour, the writing and the lines – is the most interesting?

COACHEE: The lines, I think.

COACH: Tell me some more about the lines.

COACHEE: They're spinning.'

COACH: What else do you notice about the lines?

COACHEE: They're spinning towards me.

COACH: Thank you. What else do you notice?

COACHEE: It was spinning faster that time.

COACH: Which is more interesting, the speed of the spin or the direction?

COACHEE: The direction.

COACH: Tell me which way this one spins.

COACHEE: Towards me. The top was spinning towards me.

COACH: And this one?'

COACHEE: Backwards.

COACH: And this one?

COACHEE: To the left.

In the conversation of Example 10 there are three aspects of asking questions that follow interest

- Identifying what could be of interest ('Tell me what you notice about . . .', 'Tell me what else you notice . . .')
- Selecting a more specific interest ('You've mentioned x, y and z. Which is most interesting?')
- Funnelling down: getting more specific ('Tell me some more about y.')

Translate that sequence into a work environment. This time let us take an informal coaching situation in the workplace (see Example 11). Imagine two colleagues in the office canteen for a quick coffee.

Example 11: Informal coaching in the workplace

LINDA: Hi. How's it going?

GEORGE: Terrible, now that you ask.

LINDA: Really?

GEORGE: Yes. We've just taken a break from our sales team meeting and it's going horribly wrong.

LINDA: Do you want to talk about it for a minute?

GEORGE: If you don't mind. It would be helpful.

LINDA: Tell me in what way it's going wrong.

[Identifying what could be of interest]

GEORGE: In quite a few ways. We are way behind on the agenda and Paul and Frank are at each other's throats – again.

LINDA: Anything else?

GEORGE: Maybe. The atmosphere is a bit strange.

LINDA: You've mentioned three things: being behind on the agenda, Paul and Frank, and the atmosphere. Which would be most useful to tackle first?

[Selecting a more specific interest]

GEORGE: The atmosphere. I had it on my mind as I left the meeting, but even so I think there may be something in it.'

LINDA: Tell me about the atmosphere.

[Funnelling down]

GEORGE: Well, it's not just Paul and Frank. The others are acting up too.

LINDA: What specifically do you mean by 'acting up'?

GEORGE: Snapping at each other, complaining, and not listening to each other. They're all a bit tired. It's been a long haul.

LINDA: If you could change that, would it help?

GEORGE: Yes. A lot.

LINDA: What could you do?

GEORGE: I could give them feedback on their behaviour and see if they wanted to change.

LINDA: Are you going to do that?

GEORGE: Yes, definitely.

LINDA: Do you want to talk about the other issues now – the agenda and Paul and Frank?

GEORGE: Maybe we could talk about Paul and Frank when we've got more time. As for the agenda, the reason we're behind is because of the way everyone's been behaving. Thanks.

Asking questions that follow interest is a way of enabling the coachee to move forward as a function of their own thinking and choices. It is non-directive coaching at its best. In following interest, the coachee becomes very focused, allowing full access to his or her imagination and intuition.

Questions that clarify

The W questions – 'what', 'who', 'where' and 'when' – are all useful in raising awareness. Notice that I have not included 'why'. I'll come back to that shortly.

'What', or better still 'What specifically is that' is useful when someone uses a word, a noun, that you have not come across before. For example, a coachee might state, 'I have tried hard to get the cross-tackle to work,' and a coach might respond, 'What specifically is a cross-tackle?' 'What' is similarly useful when a coachee uses a recognised word in an unrecognised context – for instance some special technical jargon or slang.

In most meetings it would not be the end of the world if you did not understand a particular word. You would merely wait for a suitable break and ask a trusted colleague. In a coaching session, where what drives the session is understanding, you simply cannot afford to miss the meaning.

'Who' is useful in two ways. The first way to use it is when someone uses a pronoun (he, she, they, it) and you are not sure who is being referred to ('Let me just check that. Who specifically made that statement? And to whom?'). The second way is to get a complete list of all the characters that might have impact on the topic of the coaching conversation ('Who else is involved?', 'Who are the other members of the team?').

'Where' and 'when' give specific location to an event in time and place, therefore be used to clarify vagueness in time (*Coachee*: 'I'll talk to Paul soon.' *Coach*: 'When exactly?') or place (*Coachee*: 'I am completely stuck with this report.' *Coach*: 'Where exactly in the report are you stuck?')

But why not 'Why'? Well, because. The 'Why' question more often then not elicits reasons, justifications and excuses, not one of which is useful in raising awareness. 'Why' does not create distance. Furthermore, 'Why' is a pretty sloppy question, for it can mean so many things – from what is your purpose, to what is your reason, to blame (as in 'But why?'). So ask a more specific question instead, such as:

- 'What is your purpose in that?'
- 'What were the reasons behind that decision?'
- 'What is it that makes that important for you?'

Questions that tie things down

One of the mistaken impressions that people get in being introduced to the notion of non-directive coaching is that the coach has to be gentle with the coachee, that the coach cannot get tough. But tying coachees down to specifics, getting them to commit and challenging them are all part of the coach's toolkit, as shown in Example 12.

Example 12: Tie things down

COACHEE: Well, that's been a useful conversation, thanks. I'll try a couple of the things we discussed over the next few weeks.

COACH: Great. Tell me what specifically you are going to do? And by when?

[Commit]

COACHEE: I think I might have a go at giving Paul some feedback.

COACH: You sound a little unsure. What are you willing to commit to?

[Challenge]

COACHEE: I believe that I have a good relationship with Frank.

COACH: I'd like to challenge that. My observation is that you've been avoiding each other for the last three weeks and that when you have to be in the same room you constantly undermine each other.

Obviously you can only challenge when you have experience of a different reality from the one being expressed.

➡ DON'T GET STUCK, GET INTERESTED

Finally, before we move on I would like to remind you of the description of the ball-catching demonstration in Chapter 1. Peter's natural ability to catch manifested itself when he was focused, when there was no interference. It's the same for you as a coach. If you are completely focused and interested in your coachee's learning, your natural instinct to coach will manifest itself and you will ask appropriate questions.

In any case, it does not particularly matter if you make a mistake. Coaching is not an exam where you only get one chance. If a question does not work, ask another. When you are in a good relationship it does not matter. The best question I was ever asked when being coached was 'I don't know what the next question is.

Do you?'. And I did. If you're stuck your attention will be with yourself and not with the coachee. Don't get stuck, get interested.

Chapter 5
Feedback, suggestions and advice

In this chapter we move down the Spectrum of Coaching Skills described in Chapter 2 and address giving feedback, making suggestions and giving advice. Towards the end of the chapter we look briefly at the two aspects closest to the directive approach, namely instructing and telling.

➡ GIVING FEEDBACK

Unfortunately, giving and receiving feedback is optional. I know it could not be any other way, but you only have to ask two questions of people in most organisations to be very clear that there is not a whole lot of giving and receiving of feedback taking place.

The first question is: 'Have you given any feedback recently?', to which the answer is almost always 'yes'. Then you ask: 'Have you received any feedback recently?', to which the answer is invariably 'no'. If you ask these questions across an organisation, you can form a number of hypotheses. One hypothesis is that there is an incredibly well-informed person, whom you have missed because that person is locked up in the basement, who is getting all the feedback. Another hypothesis is that not much feedback is taking place. A third hypothesis – and more generous one – is that people think they are giving feedback when in fact they are alluding to something or dropping hints. Whichever is the case, the vast majority of us do not receive sufficient feedback in our working relationships.

This is an important issue. This body–mind is a cybernetic system; it requires feedback from its environment in order to function properly. Another example of a cybernetic system is a guided missile – a bit out of place in this book perhaps (resorting to violence is the most extreme form of command and control), but it makes the point: a guided missile requires feedback to know whether it is on target or not.

In contrast, a lack of feedback can be likened to the experience of being in a sensory deprivation chamber, or 'float tank'. A float tank is a place where the body–mind gets virtually no feedback, and it is useful to look at what happens if someone is left in such a place for too long. A float tank is a bit like a bath only bigger, usually about seven or eight feet square. It is filled to a depth of about eighteen inches with a high-density saline solution that is exactly at body temperature. It is totally enclosed; no light or sound gets in. You cannot feel anything much because you are floating, and you do not notice the water because it is exactly the same temperature as your skin. In short, your senses are deprived of all (or almost all) stimulation.

An hour spent in a float tank gives you the equivalent rest to seven hours' sleep and is a powerful rejuvenating process. It can also put the mind into an extremely receptive state. Many people have solved nagging or serious problems, or had a creative idea in a float tank. Some sports people use them in conjunction with video images, where they see images of themselves performing perfectly and, in such a receptive state, they can train the muscle memory to repeat perfect performances. All very good, so long as you do not mind smelling faintly of Epsom salts for a week.

However, if you stay in the float tank for too long, you begin to hallucinate; you make it up. There are lots of people walking around organisations who are in a sense hallucinating, and many of them are senior executives to whom nobody feels able to tell the truth. The consequence of not receiving feedback is that we invent our version of reality. Let me say it again. When people do not know what the reality is, they make it up. You know that report that a member of your team left on your desk last week, the one you've not had time to read. Your 'response' – for that is what it is – has already been interpreted by the team member: it was not good enough – hell, I'm not good enough.

Obstacles to feedback and how to overcome them

There are a number of obstacles to giving feedback. Before we look at them, have a go at Exercise 5.1 in order to see things from the perspective of your own working environment.

Exercise 5.1: Obstacles to giving feedback

Purpose: To identify the obstacles to giving feedback.

Process

1 Make a list of all the obstacles you have encountered, or imagine others encounter, to giving feedback on work practices.

At workshops it is a useful thing to do to ask people what stops them from giving feedback. A typical list includes some of these ideas

- It's not part of my job.
- If they can't do the job, they shouldn't be here.
- It's not in the culture.
- I don't have time.
- I don't have enough information.
- Who am I to judge another?
- I don't want to discourage them.
- I don't want to hurt them.

When pushed, most people will acknowledge that not giving feedback comes down to 'I don't want to hurt them'. Underneath 'I don't want to hurt them' is another issue that I think it's worth being really clear about: if I hurt you, you will not like me any more. An understandable, but hardly noble, reason for withholding feedback.

Imagine the scenario of a chair and, behind it about fifteen feet away a waste-paper basket. In the chair sits an unsuspecting volunteer. His task, the coach informs him, is to throw a ball over his head so that it lands in the basket. It must go straight in and not bounce in – and no looking. The coach's job is to give the volunteer feedback, and the dialogue goes something like that in

Example 13.

Example 13: Ball-in-basket blind: no feedback

[The coachee throws a ball]

COACH: You missed.

COACHEE: Really.

COACH: Have another go.

[Another attempt]

COACH: You missed again.

COACHEE: By how much?

COACH: Listen, sunshine, I'm in a hurry. Get on with it.

[Another attempt]

COACH: That was even worse.

COACHEE: What do you want me to do?

COACH: Just get the ball in the basket. I suppose it's worth another try

[Eventually in exasperation the coachee throws the ball at the coach.]

The conversation in the scenario of Example 13 is noticeable for:

- the judgmental attitude of the coach
- the coach's lack of belief in the coachee's ability
- the coach making no attempt to create a relationship
- no usable data from the coach.

Imagine now that the coach has learned her lesson and is trying again. The dialogue is given in Example 14.

Example 14: Ball-in-basket blind: feedback

COACH: Thanks for volunteering. It's David, isn't it?

DAVID: Yes.

COACH: The exercise remains the same, and I'm wondering what you would like me to do to help.

DAVID: I'd like some real feedback.

COACH: And what exactly would you like from me?

DAVID: I'd like to know how far the ball was from the basket.

COACH: OK. And anything else?

DAVID: I guess you could tell me if it landed in front or behind the basket. And on which side.

COACH: OK. In front or behind and the side. How should I tell you how far away?

DAVID: What do you mean?

COACH: Feet, feet and inches, metres, that sort of thing.

DAVID: Oh no, I'm no good with distances. Just show me with your hands.

COACH: Ready to try?

DAVID: Yes.

[David throws]

COACH: The ball landed in front of the basket, about this much [shows with hands] and about the same distance to the left.

Within minutes David will throw a ball into the basket. This feedback conversation is noticeable for:

- a non-judgemental approach – just the data
- high-quality data
- feedback in the form that the coachee wants
- a stronger relationship
- the coach's belief in the coachee's potential [you'll have to take my word for that].

Before we go any further I want to put something to bed. There is no such thing as 'negative feedback' and there is no such thing as 'positive feeback'. There is just feedback. Data. What often happens is that people attach a judgement to the data to suit their purpose in that moment, and that purpose is usually 'to be right'. Then the receiver tends to respond to the judgement and not to the data – for instance, 'The boss is angry, so I won't do that again' is not a great way of getting to a good decision, but it happens with a response to a judgement. In contrast, the role of the coach is to give the data as cleanly as possible, so the coachee can receive it, assess it, and make his or her own decision as to how to proceed.

That said, in giving feedback it is near-impossible to communicate only the data. The receiver will also get some sense of your intent and the emotional charge that you carry. Let's break this concept down somewhat:

- *Data*. This needs to be of the highest quality that you can muster. It also needs to be something that you yourself have observed – second-hand information frustrates people because they cannot effectively challenge it. Specific examples help. Keep comments free from judgement and interpretation.

- *Intent*. You must be really clear about your intention in giving the feedback. If it is to prove yourself right or to get one up on the receiver, it will not work. The only intent that has integrity is to raise awareness.

- *Emotional charge*. Are you angry, disappointed or elated? Whatever your emotions, they will communicate themselves to the coachee to some degree – you simply cannot help it. It is useful to acknowledge this explicitly, so that you can manage yourself and the relationship better.

Giving feedback in everyday working life

A manager who coaches will use feedback in at least two ways. The first is as part of the everyday working life of the organisation and the other is within a coaching session. There is a useful three-step process to remember for giving feedback in the course of everyday working life:

- *Contract*. This refers to the agreement you make with the person to whom you wish to give feedback. Ideally the contract includes the elements of 'offer' ('I have got some feedback for you. Do you want it? Is this a good time/place? If not when/ where?') and clarity of intent ('I want to make sure you are successful in running these meetings.').

- *Data*. This should be the highest quality possible as observed and owned by you, and without judgement or interpretation. If it is a

weighty matter, then you might ask the coachee to self-assess:
'How do you see it?'

- *Action*. What is the coachee going to do as a result of the
  feedback? If they require further coaching, then do not assume
  that you are necessarily the coach. Coachees always have a right
  to choose their coach.

Giving feedback in a coaching session

Many of the guidelines suggested above hold true for giving
feedback in a coaching session. It is still important that the coach
does not make an assumption that the coachee will welcome the
feedback. If the session has been run in a non-directive fashion and
– suddenly and uninvited – the coach comes out with some
feedback, it can be very disruptive to the session and can damage
the relationship. And without any adequate relationship, coaching
cannot happen. The key is to offer the feedback, signalling clearly
that this is a change of style, and once the feedback has been
delivered, to move back into the non-directive mode. For instance:
'I've got some feedback for you do you want it? What I have
noticed is . . . How does that fit in with what you've been saying? Is
that worth considering?'

I have occasionally had a coachee say 'no' when I have offered
feedback. When that happens, it is almost always because they are
busy thinking through another part of the issue and do not want
that process interrupted. When they are ready, I give the feedback.
If they do not want it, do not give it.

If a pattern emerges where a coachee is continually refusing
feedback, then the coach might give feedback on the continual
refusing.

➡ MAKING SUGGESTIONS

In the context of coaching, suggestions are ideas that a coach has
that may be appropriate to the coachee's situation. They arise in
the coach's mind as a function of his or her experience, intelligence, intuition or imagination. They are occasionally valid and
occasionally acceptable to the coachee.

As with feedback, the only issue is whether the coach can present them to the coachee in such a way as to give the coachee a genuine choice as to whether or not to accept them. The issue of choice can be influenced by a number of factors: the coach's power in the relationship and ability to influence, as well as the coachee's desire to be influenced or not to have to take responsibility.

There is a complexity here that no amount of words written can completely resolve, so let us return to what is possible in practice. The guidelines are not dissimilar to those for offering feedback:

- Always present your suggestions as an offer ('I've got a suggestion. Would you like to hear it?')
- When the suggestion has been heard, return to the non-directive approach ('Does that work for you?' or 'We've identified a number of suggestions, namely w, x, y and the one I threw in, z. Which of those is the most promising?')

➡ GIVING ADVICE

I have some problems with offering advice in a coaching session. It seems to me that offering advice suggests that the coachee and the coach do not see the situation from the same viewpoint. 'Advice' suggests that the coach has not really been helpful in taking the coachee through the Reality stage of the GROW model. When I give advice, I am trying to make a stand for what *I* believe in and have probably stopped attending to the coachee's learning. So I tend not to give it.

I am, of course, presenting a rather narrow interpretation of 'advice'. If you find yourself in the position of giving advice, the guidelines are the same as for any time you move from a non-directive mode. Make an offer and, if the advice is wanted, give it. Once it has been heard, return to the non-directive coaching mode so the coachee is left with choice.

➡ INSTRUCTING AND TELLING

Giving instruction

Giving instruction is sometimes appropriate in coaching sessions. What the situation implies is that there is a technique that the coach knows and that the coachee could not work out, or that would take more time for the coachee to work out than is available. As a tennis coach, I knew quite a bit about how to play tennis, the proper technique and way of doing it. Mostly, it just got in the way of the coachee's learning.

These are times when instructions might be appropriate:

- when the coachee is tired
- when there is significant time pressure
- when the coachee is upset or panicking
- when the technique is complex (but known to the coach).

If you must give instructions, get permission to do it first and then return to the non-directive mode. In my experience, 99 per cent of the times when I have resorted to giving instructions it is because I, as the coach have lost my way in the session, or lost interest or was just too tired.

Telling

All that I have said about feedback, advice and instructions applies to telling. The reality, of course, is that you can tell anyone to do anything, but they just may not do it.

Some people may sometimes do what you say, but that may be because either they have surrendered their power to you or they are unwilling to challenge your right to tell. In either case we could not call it a coaching session.

Very occasionally, I have told people what to do in a coaching session, but always with explicit permission. And, as far as I can remember, it is always when the coachee is so overwhelmed that he needs another to take control for a short while. And that is OK as long as the coach does not then create some kind of dependency on the coach by the coachee.

➡ **A FINAL THOUGHT**

At a certain level it does not matter what the coach does in a coaching session – ask questions, make suggestions, read the telephone book – the question that needs to be asked about anything a coach might do in a coaching session is *did it raise awareness in the coachee*? That is the crux of the issue.

Chapter 6
Creativity and looking to the future

Creativity is a vital part of coaching. It is what allows the coachee to break out of a difficult situation, invent a new future or possibility, and make a step change in productivity or quality of life. It shows up in many ways, but the three that we will focus on her are concerned with creating the future (visioning and goal setting), innovation (new ways of doing things, new options) and generating success criteria.

In many of my coaching sessions I am guilty of accepting what is apparently reasonable, in the sense of what could reasonably be achieved. For instance, when a coachee is creating a vision for a career, in my mind I very often have an idea of what is possible for that person, what they are capable of achieving. And that set of judgements shows up in the session and has the potential to limit it. What is even more worrying is that my idea of what the coachee is capable of is often greater than theirs is.

The same thing can happen in the Options stage of the GROW model. The coachee comes up with a list of options that are within the confines of what is reasonable and the coach goes along with it. Now, I am not an adherent to that school of thought that says whatever you can dream of you can have; there are some things that limit us – at least at this stage of our evolution. But I am absolutely certain that there is much much more available to us if only we dare look.

I use the words 'create the future' with some resistance because I know that there are people who think the world is the way it is, that their lot is either predetermined or delivered to them out of chaos; and they have an absolute right to that point of view although, as a coach, I may of course challenge them on it. For their own sake I would want them to be certain that it was a true belief and not an excuse that allows them to dodge their responsibility for making something of their life or to accept the current situation without having to struggle.

This chapter of the book, then, is about how we can respectfully challenge coachees – and perhaps ourselves – to look beyond what is merely reasonable in order to plumb the depths of the extraordinary.

Before we get into some of the techniques involved, it is worth considering how we go about creating the future. Most of us, most of the time, create the future from the past. It is a predictable future. If we are brave, we may push the boundaries out a bit and create some 'stretch goals'. But essentially the future we imagine for ourselves is an extrapolation of what went on before. We create the future as a function of our previous experience: what worked and what did not work, our likes and dislikes, our strengths and weaknesses, our successes and failures. Unconscious processes also create needs that demand to be fulfilled. Parents, family and cultural background all play their part.

You have to be strong and courageous to do something different – and that is after you have given yourself permission to even imagine something different. The funny thing is that the people who are supposed to have our interests closest to heart are sometimes the people who do the most to ensure that we conform ('But, dear, we have always thought you would become a doctor, just like your father. Why would you ever want to be a footballer?').

So is there another way of creating the future? Ultimately, not really, because it is almost impossible to imagine something that has not had existence. The question revolves around whether or not you are willing to be constrained by the past. Can you free yourself sufficiently to create a future that is worth hanging around for, that demands your best efforts? You know what they say: be careful what you ask for, because you may get it.

➡ **CREATING THE FUTURE**

Before going further, tackle Exercise 6.1 in order to project yourself into the future and give yourself some vision of what you might then be like as a manager and coach.

Exercise 6.1: **A vision for a manager/coach**

Purpose: To create a vision for yourself as a manager who coaches.

Process

1 Cast yourself into the future, to the point where you are successful as a manager/coach. How are you spending your time? List specific ideas.

2 What are the beliefs and values you espouse? List them.

3 How would you describe your relationships with those you manage/coach?

4 How would those you manage/coach describe you?

5 What is your impact in the workplace? At home? Set down your ideas.

Now that you have created something of a vision of the future for yourself, let us turn our attention to helping coachees do the same. There are a number of techniques that I have found helpful.

The first is the most simple. Agree a time-frame that makes sense to the coachee (for example the year-end, one year's time, five years, to retirement). Ask the coachee to think of all the things that might be possible for them in that time-frame. Ask them to suggest as many ideas as they can. That done, ask them to edit the list to what is desirable.

An alternative approach is to have the coachee write a speech that would be given at the completion point of the vision: retirement, the end of a project, New Years's Day etc. What would be the successes and accomplishments that had occurred by then? Instead of, or as well as, that verbal description, have the coachee draw a picture of the vision. This can either be abstract, free drawing or a more figurative picture.

A final approach is to have the coachee close their eyes and relax, and to allow an image for the vision to come to them. The first image is usually the most useful. The coachee can then either describe the image to you, write a verbal description, or draw a picture of it.

➡ INNOVATION OR 'GETTING UNSTUCK'

It can happen in a coaching session that the coachee gets stuck and cannot see any options or possibilities or is simply looking for a new approach to a situation or problem. There are a number of ways the coach can help. The most obvious is a kind of brainstorming approach, whereby the coachee creates a list of all the possibilities available, however wild they might be. It is important that there is no evaluation of the possibilities until the list is complete or the coachee exhausted. The questions listed below can also be useful in helping the coachee to 'think outside the box':

1. 'What's the most outrageous option you can think of?'

2. 'If you could have it any way, regardless of any constraints, how would you have it?'

3. 'If you had a magic wand, what would you do?'

For example, I once worked with a team of Safety Officers on a construction site and one particular conversation was focused on how to reduce injuries among the work force. I asked the question, 'If you could do anything, regardless of cost or the time it would take, what would you do?' There were a number of suggestions and then one of the team said that he would make everyone a Safety Officer. His colleague's immediate response was to say that this would be impossible, but then remembered the rules of brainstorming and apologised. He thought for a moment and then said, 'However, we could get them to think like Safety Officers.' A simple question generated a breakthrough in the team's thinking. They no longer saw their role as one of preventing people from getting injured, which is exhausting and ultimately impossible, but rather as one of changing the mindset of the foremen.

➡ **GENERATING SUCCESS CRITERIA**

Let me tell you the story of Kevin. I was coach and manager at a small tennis centre in Ireland that was situated beside a large housing estate. The estate had been built on the outskirts of the city so as to house a former inner-city community whose original houses had been torn down to make room for office blocks and shops. As with many such developments, the uprooted community developed more than their fair share of social problems. There was a high unemployment percentage, and attendant violence, drink and drugs problems.

On one particular Friday, shortly after the schools had broken up for the summer holidays, a boy about twelve years of age appeared at the tennis centre. He watched everything that was going on and gravitated towards the court where I was working. I was coaching a client in the serve. All the balls had been hit down to the other end of the court, so I turned to collect them and almost tripped over the boy. He had collected all the balls into the basket and had brought them back to me. Without a word he then ran back to the other end of the court.

Some minutes later all the balls had been used up but the client needed to hit some more. I looked to the boy, who was at the other end of the court. He took a ball and threw it the length of the court straight into my hand. I said nothing, put the ball in my pocket and held out my hand. Thwack. Another ball, straight into the palm of my hand. I looked at the client. This frail looking boy, with a great big grin, had an elegance of technique and a rhythm that you seldom see. His name was Kevin. He had played tennis once before with an aunt. He had enjoyed it and would like to try again. He spent the rest of the day helping me during the lessons.

The next day we had a tennis lesson. He learned very quickly. It was a Saturday and there were a lot of people about. Pretty soon there was a small crowd around the court. It was not just that he had talent and a grace about his movement, but he had a joy about him that was infectious. At the end of the summer Kevin had made remarkable progress. He had also seen some of the better tennis players in his age group working out at the centre. The next year he wanted to play a few tournaments. I agreed to coach him over the winter and in exchange he was to keep tidy part of the tennis centre. In making our agreement, I asked him what his goals were. He wanted to qualify for the national championships and win his first-round match in the next year. That would have put him in the best 32 players in his age group – a stretch goal if I had ever seen one.

Kevin worked hard over the next year, often coming to the centre before school to get in some extra practice. The tennis centre had never been so tidy. Unbelievably, he qualified for the nationals. I had a business meeting when his first-round match was on and did not get to see it. I got to the club just as the result was posted. He had won. It took me some time to find him. He was in an annexe to the changing room and had been crying.

'What's wrong? You won, didn't you?'

'Yes.' His voice was shaking.

'So what's wrong?'

'It was a bad match. I felt tense the whole time. We were both angry; I could see it in his face. And I used a bad word. And he called me a bad name. I don't want to play like that.'

'So how do you want to play?'

He relaxed a little. 'I want to feel relaxed and calm, like when *we* play.'

'What else?'

'And I want to feel the ball in the centre of my racket. I want us both to be happy and smiling. And I want to be able to say "good shot" when my opponent hits a good shot.'

'Is that how you want to play your next match?'

'Yes.'

Kevin lost his next match, but it was nevertheless a great victory for him. He played beautifully and gave full expression to who he was.

Kevin's original goal was very clear by most criteria. It was specific, measurable, realistic (if a bit of a stretch) and had a clear end-date: to reach the second round of the nationals next year. But we had missed something critical and had stumbled on to an interesting additional technique in resolving it. When Kevin told me what had gone wrong and then translated it into how he wanted it to be, everything was described in terms of things that he could either see, hear or feel. When you think about it, if you cannot detect something through your senses, then it does not exist for you; it is a figment of your imagination. If you take the time to translate goals or objectives into what you can see hear and feel – and, I guess, smell, if you must – then you will identify two additional aspects of the goal: an additional set of measures, and clarity that the goal as expressed is the goal that the coachee wants. These two aspects can guard against the danger hinted at in the saying 'Be careful of what you ask for, because you may get it.'

In a coaching session, using the technique of generating success criteria might arise in dialogue something like that in Example 15.

Example 15: Measuring success

COACH: So, what is your longer-term goal for your time management?

COACHEE: If I could get to a position, within the next month, where I am saving three hours a week, am processing less paper, and get the weekly reports out on time, that would be just great.

COACH: And when you have successfully achieved that, how will you know? What would you see that was different?

COACHEE: Three times a week I'd get home earlier.

COACH: And what would you see? What would be the evidence?

COACHEE: The evidence would be me, my body, standing in the kitchen with the clock saying six o'clock and not seven.

COACH: And what would you hear?

COACHEE: I'd hear the kids laughing and playing, because they would still be up. And, on a good day, my wife would be saying 'You're home early. That's nice.' And she'd be happy to see me.

COACH: What would you see, actually, if she was happy?

COACHEE: A smile.

COACH: And what would you feel?

COACHEE: More relaxed.

COACH: How else would you know?

. . .

Making a goal or objective as 'real' as that in Example 15 gives some clear measures, confirmation that it is the right goal, and typically deepens the desire to achieve it.

Chapter 7
Applications

The skills involved in coaching can be applied in many different ways and in many different environments, from the workplace to the schoolroom to the sports field. As you internalise the skills and make them your own, you will find that they show up in many aspects of your life.

One of the exciting things about the School of Coaching, which I have established with The Industrial Society in the United Kingdom, is watching the participants progress through the programme and report at the various workshops how what they have learned has shown up in all aspects of their life: the consultant who, having a meeting that was not progressing well with a client, was inspired to change the meeting into a coaching session; the director of training who found herself listening to her husband; the senior executive who began acknowledging the real talent and creativity that his teenage daughter possessed. For me, these are some of the truly inspiring stories from my experience, not because they are so important and meaningful – which they undoubtedly are – but because it is a real demonstration that something has changed at a very fundamental level in the participants. They have reoriented themselves in relation to others and have made their relationships more powerful.

This, however, is a book about coaching skills for managers. There are several obvious applications for coaching skills within the workplace, and it is useful to examine them. Before we do so, tackle Exercise 7.1.

Exercise 7.1: Coaching opportunities

Purpose: To identify your specific applications or opportunities for coaching.

Process

1 Make a list of all the work-related situations that you are faced with where you could use coaching.

2 Make a similar list of coaching opportunities related to sports, hobbies, family and friends.

Some of the applications of coaching are situations that are distinctly coaching sessions; others are situations in which you might be able to apply coaching skills. For example, if someone who asks for coaching on a particular matter approaches you, then that is a distinct coaching session. Alternatively, you might use some of your coaching skill during an appraisal interview or performance review. An appraisal interview is not a coaching session; it is part of the management process of the organisation to which both parties belong. The critical distinction is that in a coaching session the coachee has complete and free choice over how it progresses, whereas in an appraisal interview the manager has some authority. Ultimately the coachee *always* has choice and it is important to recognise that – it might just mean that they choose to work elsewhere!

➡ A DISTINCTION: FORMAL AND INFORMAL COACHING

Before we discuss specific applications it will be valuable to make a distinction between what could be called 'formal coaching' and 'informal coaching'. I should warn you that the distinction is not perfect, and one form can very easily become the other and both can exist at different times in a working relationship.

Formal coaching

Formal coaching involves an explicit agreement between both parties, where one person is clearly the coach and the other clearly the coachee. It may be a one-off session where there has been a request for coaching, or part of a coaching programme that takes place over time. It usually implies that the coaching topic (or topics) is of some significance or gravity. In formal coaching, the coachee always has the right to choose their coach and to stop being coached if they feel that they are moving into areas that they do not want to be in – for example, areas where counselling or therapy may be more appropriate.

Informal coaching

Informal coaching takes place as part of the general run of play. It happens between colleagues at all levels in an organisation, between peers, between a manager and his team; it does not respect hierarchy. I remember asking my then boss, just before a critical meeting, what his ideal outcome from the meeting was. One successful meeting later he acknowledged the value of the question and how it had kept us both focused in the meeting.

Informal coaching does not necessarily require a clear agreement between coach and coachee, although most relationships work better when the parties know what is expected of them. Informal coaching happens on the spur of the moment: in the staff canteen a colleague indicates that she is having a difficult time with a particular client or with some aspect of a project; a member of staff complains that he will never get a particular job done on time. Both of these are opportunities for informal coaching.

It is in situations such as these that the manager who coaches shows up most clearly and can have a profound and lasting effect on the performance and learning of his subordinates. And, frankly, it is a significantly more rewarding way of doing business. In a formal coaching session I know that I am being coached and have agreed to it; in an informal coaching conversation I may not know that I am being coached – I just know that someone is trying to help me.

➡ SOME USEFUL APPLICATIONS

Here, then, is a list of some of the principal applications:

- Coaching subordinates
- coaching within the management processes
- coaching within a training programme
- coaching as part of leadership
- coaching on projects
- coaching upwards
- coaching peers
- mentoring
- coaching your partner
- coaching children
- self-coaching.

Coaching subordinates

The most obvious of all applications in the workplace is that of a manager coaching those who report to her or him, whether in the formal or informal sense. As I have said earlier, coaching where there is a line-management relationship presents some difficulties in that the coach–manager has some power in the face of which it can be difficult to create an environment of trust. Another difficulty is that the coachee may simply want to be directed, and may not want to have to think or to take responsibility. I suggest that these difficulties are not insurmountable and should be treated as obstacles to be overcome with patience and imagination.

Coaching within the management processes

Most organisations run a number of management processes that lend themselves to coaching – in particular the people-management processes such as performance reviews, appraisals, development reviews, objective-setting meetings and progress reviews.

It staggers me that there are still organisations nowadays where the manager sets the subordinate's goals. I can think of few quicker, more sure-fire ways of eroding motivation and undermining responsibility. Most organisations are more enlightened than that, and allow for self-assessment on the part of the subordinate, including self-identification of goals. Such self-assessment and self-identification are perfect set-pieces for some coaching. If you are unfortunate enough to work for an organisation where the process suggests that the manager does the assessment and sets the goals, then I propose that you do what you know works.

Coaching within a training programme

Coaching can be used to great effect to ensure that someone gets full value from a training programme. The manager or trainer can coach a delegate prior to the event so that the delegate is very clear about the learning objectives. When the event is completed, a further coaching session can consolidate the learning and ensure that it gets applied in the workplace to best effect.

Coaching as part of leadership

Effective leadership is so dependent on the personality of the leader and the followers, the culture of the organisation, and the nature of the business that I am not going to be foolish enough to make a statement about good leadership. What I will say is that when there is an alignment between what inspires an individual, the job they are doing and the direction of the company, then people at all levels can give of their best freely, communication becomes easier and phenomenal results can accrue. A coaching approach that directly involves staff in the direction the business is taking and the shape of their job can be part of what creates that alignment.

Coaching on projects

There are two ways in which coaching is appropriate to delivering projects. One is where the leader of the project has some line authority, and the second is where there is a coach appointed who has no line relationship. They can be from inside the business, from another department, or external to it.

In the situation where the coach is also the project leader with management responsibility, the same problems arise for coaching a team as occur for a manager coaching one-on-one. I talk about this in Chapter 8 (common pitfalls). In the situation where the coach has no line authority, there is the potential for conflict with the project leader. Again, this issue is considered later in the book, in Chapter 9 on coaching teams.

Coaching upwards

'Is it possible to coach my boss?' is a question frequently asked at coaching-skills workshops. The answer is, of course, that anyone can be coached – if they are willing. What is interesting, I think, is what is behind the question – which is usually a different question: 'How can I change my boss's behaviour?' To that question there is a different answer: you cannot change anyone else's behaviour; only they can.

What you can do, though, is give them some feedback. If they are willing to listen to the feedback and understand it, then coaching may be appropriate. After that, they have the right to choose their coach, which may or may not be the person giving the feedback. In my experience, it is unusual for a boss to be willing to be coached by a subordinate, but it is not unheard-of. When it happens, it is a tremendously powerful signal that the boss is truly open to learning and to meaningful communication, the impact of which extends well beyond the person who initially volunteered the feedback.

The scenario above fits into my fairly loose definition of formal coaching. Coaching upwards in the informal sense can happen much more easily and frequently, but it is dependent on the prevailing culture in the organisation and just how much of a control-junkie the person 'upwards' of you is.

Coaching peers

Coaching between friends and within a peer group is perhaps the easiest environment in which to coach, in the sense that there are the fewest obstacles to an effective relationship. This is because it is less likely than with a line relationship that there are competing agendas or that the coach has an investment in the outcome (other than that the session should be successful, which is an obstacle in itself).

Some organisations have instituted a system of 'buddy coaching' or co-coaching. The notion here is that two people who have some training in coaching skills support each other in the pursuit of performance or learning objectives. As you might imagine, some of the pairings meet once or twice and then the pressures of work override the initial good intentions. Other pairings maintain the practice even when the individuals move on to other parts of the business or to other countries, resorting to the phone for their coaching fix. I know of at least one case where the buddy-coaching relationship persisted after both protagonists had moved to new companies.

Mentoring

I tried in Chapter 2 to make a distinction between coaching and mentoring, suggesting that in principle mentoring was more concerned with longer-term career issues whereas coaching was more concerned with nearer-term performance issues.

The point to be made here is that the models, tools and skills that are critical to coaching, as I have described them, will also enable more effective mentoring to take place. A mentor who is reliant on, say, an avuncular style and dependent on having had significant experience of the organisation, of business and of life in general may well provide great benefit and be a wonderful person to be with. However, at the very least such a mentor would need to be able to listen effectively in order to ensure that the pearls of wisdom were indeed pearls in the eyes of the mentee. On a still more positive note, a mentor who has vast experience and can use it to good effect and who can also employ a non-directive approach when appropriate will have much greater impact.

Coaching your partner

'Don't do your professional stuff on me!' Ouch! Effective coaching requires that there is a relationship where the coach can separate himself from the outcome and from what is going on for the coachee. In a relationship where two people have a commitment to each other and whose lives have become entwined, such a separation is often difficult and sometimes virtually impossible.

However, while acknowledging that there are some quite tough obstacles to creating an effective coaching relationship within, say, a marital relationship, it is not impossible to give and receive coaching and may even be a sign of a healthy and mature relationship. The key is to identify and talk about the obstacles before doing any coaching.

Coaching children

In my relationship with my stepdaughter, Victoria, my coaching skills have played an important part, particularly when it comes to homework. When she gets stuck with something, the truth is that she probably knows more about the topic than I, so helping her think it through is the most valuable assistance I can give. I also happen to believe that the homework is for *her* to do and not me, so if I use coaching she gets to write her own essay by using her *own* prolific imagination. Coaching and all the skills involved have a wonderful place in the relationship with children. In the teenage years, where at times nothing seems to work, the least you can do is listen.

Coaching yourself

In a sense, you are coaching yourself all the time. When you take your nose out of this book to ponder some point, be it a new insight or a disagreement, it could be argued that you are coaching yourself. When you take time out to consider a project you are engaged in or say to yourself 'Hold on – how do I really want this to be?' you are coaching yourself. Some of the most valuable time that I spend on behalf of my clients is when I take the dog for a walk – I just have not yet found a way of charging for it.

However, there are limitations to a person's ability to coach themselves. Coaching is about raising awareness and therefore, if I consider an issue on my own and in isolation, at a certain level I will be trapped by my own patterns of thought. From the inside I cannot see me. Part of why coaching works is because, in that moment when the coachee communicates to another and is understood, the thoughts are externalised and a certain distance is achieved between the coachee and their thoughts and emotions.

There are some techniques that you can use to externalise your thoughts and achieve some objectivity. For instance, a former colleague tells the story of an argument he had with his wife. At some point, in desperation, he left the house, as he tells it 'letting the front door do the talking'. Once outside on the pavement, he brought his breathing into focus and relaxed somewhat. He then proceeded to coach himself. He walked, first, on the left-hand side of the pavement and from this position he was coach and asked questions. Having asked a question, he then moved to the right-hand side of the pavement from which place, as coachee, he answered the questions. While this was difficult for other pavement users and upsetting for the neighbours (who might well have thought him to be drunk as he weaved his way around the block), my colleague achieved some resolution in his mind to the problem.

Another technique that works quite well is to write your thoughts down on paper, using the GROW model to structure the ideas.

Chapter 8
Implementation

Learning the skills of coaching is a relatively easy task, and in a workshop situation most people can achieve a high level of skill in two days. The problems arise when they get back to their place of work, where busyness, the prevailing culture, and the expectations of co-workers, boss and subordinates, tend to undermine the good intentions expressed at the end of the workshop.

In this sense, then, this chapter is the most important part of the book. Of course the skills are important but I suggest that even a relatively unskilled coach whose heart is in the right place is a lot better than having no coaching taking place at all. (Now that I think of it, I am not sure it is possible to be a 'bad' coach if your heart is in the right place.)

This chapter covers a number of topics, as follows:

- seven ways to get started
- some common obstacles
- common pitfalls
- the coaching relationship
- a typical coaching programme.

Implementing coaching in teams or projects is discussed in Chapter 9.

Before we look at the details of implementation, have a try at Exercise 8.1.

Exercise 8.1: **Getting started**

Purpose: To consider how to start coaching in the workplace.

Process

1 List the ways in which you could engage people (subordinates, peers, boss) in coaching.

2 What are the obstacles to you applying coaching in your workplace? List them down.

3 In what ways could you overcome the obstacles you have identified? List these down.

➡ SEVEN WAYS TO START COACHING

The approaches that are outlined below are written with a business manager in mind. They are not the only ways of beginning coaching, but they are simply some tried and tested methods and many of them can be used in combination. Later in the chapter I will flesh the ideas out still further when describing a full coaching programme.

Using feedback as the starting point

This is perhaps the easiest and least complicated way of bringing coaching into the workplace. To introduce coaching in this way requires that there is some real and substantive feedback to be given, and by this I mean that the situation is not something the receiver of the feedback can change simply and immediately. Assuming this is the case, when the manager has successfully given feedback (see Chapter 5), support in the form of coaching can then be offered. If the coaching is seen to work, it is a relatively simple task to introduce other topics into the agenda.

If the coaching continues to be a success, it is important to formalise the coaching relationship (see later in this chapter).

Via the appraisal or performance review

As I suggested earlier in Chapter 7, appraisals and performance reviews are ideal situations in which to begin to coach. The outcomes from such events are likely to include a set of objectives for the subordinate to pursue, most of which will be suitable topics for coaching. This is another ideal opportunity for the manager to offer coaching. It has an advantage over many other ways of introducing coaching, in that the prospective coachee will have experienced coaching already in the meeting and will have some sense of what it involves.

As with using feedback as the starting point, it is important to formalise the coaching relationship as soon as possible.

Via a team agreement

This is perhaps the most effective way to introduce coaching, and it assumes that the manager has a team of people reporting to him or her. It involves bringing the team together for a meeting that, at a minimum, would have the following outcomes:

- a collective understanding of what coaching is, including the notions of non-directive coaching and formal and informal coaching

- agreement about how specifically to get started – for example, setting in place individual programmes, starting with the next performance reviews, etc.

- the ground rules for coaching, which should include an agreement about confidentiality and possibly also discussion about how topics get onto the coaching agenda, the timing and frequency of meetings, the use (or otherwise) of formal and/or informal coaching, and how to give feedback to the coach.

It is a good idea to give a coaching session with a willing team member during the team meeting, because this is the most direct way of communicating what coaching is. The volunteer coachee must choose a real topic to be coached on; otherwise the demonstration will not work. The beauty of this approach is that it is explicit and agreed to and, because of that easily allows open discussion on the effectiveness of the coaching approach and the manager's proficiency.

The meeting can be facilitated by an external coach, which allows the manager to participate fully.

The following are possible agenda items for such a team meeting:

- *To describe the purpose of the meeting and the desired outcomes.* A coach would also ask if there were any other outcomes the group wanted.

- *To define coaching.* Exercise 2.1 would be a useful way into the discussion, getting people to share the experiences of effective and ineffective coaching. The definition of coaching given in Chapter 2 might also help.

- *To demonstrate a coaching session.* First describe the GROW model and then demonstrate it with a willing volunteer. It is a good idea to identify the volunteer before hand and to make sure they have a real issue to be coached on. Set a time limit for the session: 20 minutes is about as much as spectators can manage. After the session, review it in the group.

- *To discuss with the team what the applications of coaching might be.* Exercise 7.1 might help with this. Out of all the possible applications, agree with the team which ones are appropriate and how the team might get started.

- *To ask what ground rules would help in making the coaching effective.* Make sure that the issues of confidentiality and feedback to the coach get discussed.

Via an individual agreement

It follows, of course, that pretty much the same approach that I have described for introducing coaching via teams can be used on a one-to-one basis. The initial meeting in the coaching programme outlined later in this chapter describes how to get one-to-one coaching started in detail.

There is a distinct advantage in taking an individual approach, and this is that the individual may feel more at ease without any colleagues present. On the other hand, some of the power of collective agreement and commitment gained by using the team approach is lost. My recommendation would be to do both; to have a team meeting followed by a series of individual meetings.

Via practice clients

At the School of Coaching, the participant works with 'practice clients' for the duration of the programme. Practice clients are people with a real interest in being coached who understand that the coach is still in training. This takes the pressure to perform – to 'get it right' – off the trainee coach to some degree and sets the scene for more relaxed coaching sessions in which the coach can get quality feedback from the practice-client coachee. This is a powerful way for a manager to introduce coaching while continuing to learn. Maybe all sessions should be viewed as practice sessions, because in that atmosphere of mutuality and playfulness both parties make the most progress.

I notice that coaches often feel that they have to do it right all the time and that they cannot make mistakes. What nonsense! As long as a coach has a strong relationship with a coachee, the coach should feel free to try new things and get it wrong – all in the service of the coachee. If the coach does indeed handle a situation incorrectly, an acknowledgement to that effect and a second try is the way to progress.

Alongside tasks, projects or change programmes

Introducing coaching in order to help individuals or teams to achieve important tasks or projects, or to see through the delivery of a change initiative, is arguably the most successful route to implementing coaching. It makes it clear that coaching is not some new touchy-feely trend in the organisation. Rather, it puts coaching in its proper context: performance and learning. At the time when the individual or the team is being offered the opportunity to perform a new task, the manager should be offering coaching support.

➡ COMMON PITFALLS

There are a number of pitfalls that the inexperienced coach can fall into, as set out here.

When the coachee is seen to be failing

It is very difficult to coach successfully in a 'remedial' situation, and I use the word 'remedial' very deliberately because that is often how organisations – or people in organisations – hold it when a staff member is seen to be failing.

One of the reasons people fail in organisations is because the organisation has let them down. Of course I do not want to take the responsibility away from the individual, and if an individual is failing when they need to take responsibility for that and take some action. But in any relationship – and I include the relationship between a staff member and an organisation – there is 100 per cent responsibility for the relationship on both sides. I do know that that makes 200 per cent.

There are two reasons in particular to be cautious in these circumstances. Firstly, the organisation may already have rejected the coachee but has not admitted it. In this case, even if the coaching is successful, the organisation may be unable or unwilling to readmit the coachee. Secondly, the coachee may already have rejected the organisation and, again, not admitted it.

I have frequently been called into situations by clients where the prospective coachee is deemed to be failing. The problem is often that the coachee has not been given feedback early enough (if at all), or that the manager has been unwilling to bite the bullet and have the difficult conversation with the member of staff. As a result, the organisation gets an executive coach in to sort it.

The most useful thing that can be done in these situations is to get the relevant manager, or the Human Resources Department, to have a frank conversation with the 'failing' employee so that all parties know where they stand. After that, coaching may be possible, but I would want everyone to know that a possible outcome from the coaching would be that the coachee might decide to leave the organisation.

Who is the client?

Whether you are an external executive coach or a manager within an organisation, when you engage in coaching you need to be very clear as to who 'the client' is. Many people, particularly external coaches, believe it to be the person they are coaching. This may be the case, but more commonly it is a senior executive (who is authorising the work – and paying the bills) or even the full Board.

It's not therapy

Sometimes it seems to me that a good listener creates a vacuum – a silence – that others feel compelled to fill. And as the speaker (the coachee) notices that what they are saying is not being evaluated or judged, they begin to demonstrate trust in the relationship. So they say some more; they say things that they would never dream of saying under other circumstances. The things that taxi drivers have said to me are beyond belief (and, in some cases, repetition).

It happens occasionally in coaching sessions that the coachee broaches a topic – because they trust the coach – that may well be better handled by a counsellor or therapist (see Chapter 2). If this happens, the coach should abandon the process of coaching, but not that of listening, and refer the coachee to a counsellor or therapist.

➡ THE COACHING RELATIONSHIP

Effective coaching rests on a solid relationship between coach and coachee. It seems such an obvious thing – too obvious to have to write it down – but the truth is that the only thing that can cause coaching to fail is an insufficiently strong relationship. As a practising coach and a supervisor of other people's development as coaches, I notice that almost every unsuccessful coaching intervention is the result of a ropy relationship.

Coaching fails when something is left unsaid. The relationship has to be sufficiently strong for the coachee to trust in the coach and feel safe – to feel safe enough to say whatever is on his or her mind, to own up to mistakes and weaknesses, to suggest the absurd or the impossible; in a word, to be vulnerable. In fact, it is considerably more than that. The coachee must feel free to challenge the coach and to give feedback – to say 'This isn't working,' or 'I don't understand the question,' or 'No, I don't want to consider that option yet. This one is more interesting.'

I want you to be clear that to have a good coaching relationship does not necessarily mean that you have to like the coachee. Sure, it helps when the two of you are going to be locked away in a room for an hour together, but that is not what does it. *Trust* does it and I can have that with someone that I do not like. The practical, mechanistic aspects of establishing a good coaching relationship are dealt with in the next chapter. Here I would like to discuss what underpins that relationship.

The qualities of a good coaching relationship include:

- trust
- honesty
- openness
- transparency

Trust

The coachee needs to be able to trust the coach fully. The coachee needs to trust that whatever is said will not be repeated to anyone else; to trust that thoughts, beliefs, fears and ideas will be respected and not ridiculed; to trust in the coach's intention to be of real assistance; and to trust that the information elicited in the session will not be used to evaluate the coachee or the coachee's performance.

Equally, the coach needs to be able to trust in the coachee – to trust that the coachee is fully engaged in getting value, and is being as truthful as possible.

Honesty

The coachee needs to be honest in telling it as he really sees it or believes it to be, in taking responsibility for his actions, perceptions and beliefs. And the coach needs to be honest with the coachee.

This latter aspect is a more difficult one, because a coachee will occasionally ask for the coach's opinion – and the opinion is likely to include some judgement or assessment. Judgement and assessment do not fit easily with a non-judgemental, non-directive coaching style. And yet there is a need to be honest. So if the coach is asked for an opinion, the first thing to do is to find out why the coachee requires the opinion. Very often asking the question 'For what reason do you want my opinion?' will allow the coachee to see that they were looking for reassurance, and once that has been understood they may no longer require the coach's opinion.

Another tack to take is to turn the request back to the coachee as in 'I'll give you my opinion if you want it. But before I do, tell me what your own point of view is.' If, after both of these questions, the coachee still wants the coach's opinion, then he might choose to give it. I am usually quite willing to express a point of view on a plan of action, an idea or behaviour. I would resist responding to a question such as 'What do you think of me?' and challenge why the coachee wanted to know. After all, it is just my 'stuff' and I am not there to pass judgement. My judgement has no real validity or currency in the relationship.

Openness

Openness is obviously critical in the coaching relationship. And coaches need to recognise that that quality is the most hard-earned – even more so than honesty. Coaching requires complete honesty, but only requires 'appropriate' openness. 'Appropriate' means here that all the information that the coachee possesses – all the thoughts, ideas and beliefs that are needed to make progress on the topic – are available and part of the discussion.

It is likely that the coachee will have thoughts, ideas and beliefs that he would never reveal to anyone, let alone a work colleague. Or he may simply have promised confidentiality on an issue. If a situation arises in which the coachee is unable to be open, and this is explicit (i.e. he is honest about it), then that in itself is a sign of a healthy relationship. He just may need to find another coach for that particular topic.

Transparency

Transparency means that one's intentions, within the context of the coaching, are completely clear to the other party and, almost certainly, explicitly so. Transparency is a quick way to build trust in a relationship. As a relationship develops, there is typically less need for transparency to be present explicitly, because the partners trust each other's good intentions.

Transparency in a coaching session, coming from the coach, sounds like the sentences following:

- 'My intention in giving you this feedback is to broaden your understanding.'
- 'I really did not understand what you just said. Can you say it again?'
- 'I need to understand this part better. Can you tell me about it?'
- 'I am really sorry, I lost concentration.'
- 'I'd like you to try this visioning exercise. I believe it will help clarify what you really want.'
- 'I have a suggestion for you. Do you want it?'

In the name of transparency I introduce new clients to the GROW model and the Spectrum of Coaching Styles in my first meeting with them, so that they know what I am doing in the session. To understand better the importance of transparency, just think about how *not* understanding the coach's intentions would impact the coachee. I suggest that the coachee would find it difficult to trust the coach, to be honest and appropriately open – in other words, no coaching would occur!

➡ A TYPICAL COACHING PROGRAMME

An important part of getting started is to have some idea about how a coaching programme might look. In describing a coaching programme, I am indicating a fairly formal relationship between the manager–coach and the coachee – one that takes place over a period of time and that is designed to help the coachee achieve substantial goals.

Such a programme has a number of elements, which I will describe in some detail. Not all these elements will be appropriate for every situation, and so you will need to take a pick-and-mix approach. If I tell the truth, I have probably never run a coaching programme that included all the elements described and that what actually occurs is a far more fluid and natural process. The programme may also be of help to managers who are not anticipating working with their subordinates in such a structured way.

Before I outline the elements of the programme you might like to complete the next self-coaching exercise, Exercise 8.2.

Exercise 8.2: **Designing a coaching programme**

Purpose: To identify the elements of a coaching programme.

Process: Write down your answers to the following questions:

1 What might the critical elements of a programme be?

2 What would be the key elements of any 'contract' between the coach and a coachee?

3 What sources could aid in the generation of the goals for the programme?

4 Who else might need to be involved, and how would you involve them?

The elements of a coaching programme are shown in diagram form in Figure 8.1. In essence they are as follows:

- an initial meeting
- Session 1 (goal setting) followed by ongoing coaching
- a mid-point review
- further ongoing coaching
- final review and completion.

There are other important aspects that need also to be defined and agreed. These include: a reasonably formal 'contract', or set of procedural agreements, between the coach and coachee; agreement over the frequency and duration of the coaching sessions; and how the meetings will be documented. These aspects, too, are described further in this chapter.

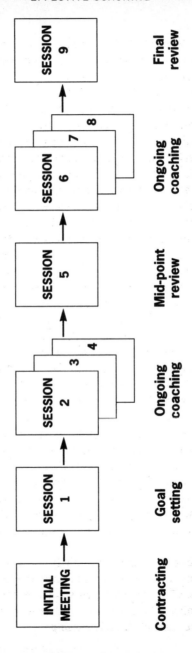

Figure 8.1: Outline of a typical coaching programme

Initial meeting

Purpose: To establish whether or not there is a need for coaching, to achieve agreement in principle for the coaching programme, to start to build relationship, and to establish the ground rules for the coaching.

Formal introductions having been achieved, the coach might suggest the foregoing as the purpose of the meeting.

An easy starting point is the coachee's background. This might include an overview of the educational and professional history and a description of their current role. The next talking point is probably the reasons why coaching is a possibility, what prompted the introduction, and what the coachee is hoping to achieve through coaching. The conversation is likely then to shift to what 'coaching' means, possibly introducing the GROW model and the Spectrum of Coaching Styles together with a description of a typical coaching programme.

At this point there will be an emerging sense that coaching is either the right way to go – or not. If it is not, have the courage to say so and support the coachee in finding what they need. If coaching does seem appropriate, then a discussion about the ground rules for the programme is next on the agenda. Issues to cover here include confidentiality, honesty, openness, feedback to the coach, and logistical issues such as venue, duration of both the whole programme and individual sessions, and guidelines for the postponement of sessions (notice required etc.).

Seek a commitment to go ahead. Remember that you have to make a commitment too, and that you need to feel confident in your ability to deliver your part of the bargain. If you are not confident, try to identify the obstacle and address it – if appropriate – with the coachee. Once agreement to proceed is in place, the coach should talk through the first session (outlined below) to identify any materials or information that are required ready for that session.

If the client for the programme (namely the person who pays the bills or has commissioned the coach) is different from the coachee, the coach and coachee should discuss how the client is to be kept informed. It is always best that the coachee is responsible for this, maintaining the trust in the relationship.

Session 1: goal setting

Purpose: To identify and agree specific goals and success measures for the programme.

The coach should declare the purpose of the session (given above) and should ask the coachee whether or not they have any additional goals for the session. Given that the coachee's needs do not change the nature of the session, the coach starts by asking the coachee what his goals are for the coaching programme. This may duplicate part of the initial meeting, in which case it will be necessary to check that the goals have not changed. Then bring into the discussion the various sources from which goals might emerge:

- the client's perception
- the coachee's manager's perception
- feedback to the coachee (e.g. 360° feedback programme)
- the coachee's current business objectives
- the coachee's career vision
- recent appraisals, performance reviews or personal development plans
- strategic initiatives and change programmes in the organisation.

All of the above may add information on the coachee's goals.

The next step is to identify the success measures for the programme (see Chapter 6). If there is a requirement to keep a third party informed, the client or the coachee's manager for instance, then sending a copy of the goals to that individual for agreement is an appropriate step.

It may be that there will be a set of public goals, and one or two private goals – only shared between the coach and coachee – where the issues are of a more personal nature. Bearing in mind the need for the coach's integrity, mentioned earlier in this chapter, the inclusion of private goals is only a legitimate practice so long as the coach and coachee are agreed that the achievement of the private goals contributes towards the coachee's productivity in the client organisation.

The final step might be to check that the goals identified are achievable in the time-frame of the coaching programme and in the number of sessions contracted to.

Session 2 and subsequent sessions

Purpose: To make progress towards the programme goals.

The coach once more declares up front the purpose of the session and asks the coachee what he wants to achieve in the session. While a principle of coaching is 'following interest', it is important that the topic(s) for the session is considered in relation to the goals for the overall programme. It is often all too compelling for the coachee to choose a topic that was the last thing in mind – for instance a recent insight or upset – and not deal with the issues that will take him towards his longer-term goals.

The topics for the session having been agreed, the actions from the previous meeting need to be reviewed. That done, each of the identified topics are worked through using the GROW model. The penultimate step in the session is to pull together the action plan (see the section in this chapter entitled 'Reports of meetings'). The final step in any session is to request feedback from the coachee.

Subsequent sessions follow the same general format as this session, with the session purpose being agreed, actions being reviewed, topics being worked through, and the final wrap-up and feedback.

Mid-programme review

Purpose: To check progress towards the programme goals and to review the coaching relationship.

Ideally, the mid-programme review will form the first part of a typical coaching session, leaving time also for some coaching in the meeting. Progress towards the programme goals is reviewed, the ground rules are reviewed, the effectiveness of the coaching is discussed, and feedback from the coachee is solicited.

Sometimes coachees are reluctant to give feedback, often because they do not want to upset the coach and run the risk of damaging an important relationship. In order to move beyond this, I find that if I reflect on the sessions before the meeting then I can usually identify a number of issues that I am not comfortable about in my own performance. If the coachee is not forthcoming with feedback, I can then ask specific questions and this will break the deadlock.

On a longer programme, it may be appropriate to seek feedback on the coachee's progress from other parties, such as the client, the coachee's manager, or some other person in the direct reporting line.

Final review and completion

Purpose: To assess progress towards the programme goals and complete the relationship.

In the final session, it is important to take the time to review the whole programme. This allows both the coachee and the coach to maximise their learning from the event and to complete the relationship. Relationships that are incomplete, that drift into separation, retain some of the emotional energy that was invested in them, and this energy is not available for other relationships or activities.

For instance, if the coachee cancels a session and then, for reasons of busyness or whatever, the session is not re-booked, the coach may spend a considerable amount of energy wondering what went wrong or if he was doing a good job. It might even undermine his confidence. The coachee, on the other hand, may be embarrassed or feeling guilty and spend time worrying about what he is going to say when he meets up with the coach. They may even try to avoid one another in the corridors.

The outline for the session is similar to the mid-programme review, as outlined above. If the client and the coachee are different people, then the client should be included in the process of completion. The coaching may end at this point, or a different relationship may emerge such as quarterly meetings. In this latter case, a restart of the programme from scratch should occur.

The contract

It is useful to have a clear – and preferably written – contract between the coach and coachee. There is no value in being too heavy handed with this and present it as if it were a legal document or for either party to feel heavily constrained; the purpose of the contract is to ensure an effective, hassle-free relationship and, like any contract, you do not need it until you do – at which point, if you do not have one it is too late.

The contract should include the programme goals, the success measures, the ground rules and, if appropriate, the fees for the programme.

Meeting duration and frequency

There are no set rules about the frequency and duration of meetings, and each coaching relationship will develop its own pattern. The place to start, as you might guess, is by asking the coachee what they would be comfortable with. Additionally, there are some factors that should be considered between the coach and coachee in developing a programme:

- the time-frame in which the goals are to be achieved
- the coachee's need for support
- the level of 'stretch' in the goals.

I find it very difficult to get anything meaningful done, when coaching in the formal sense, in anything under an hour, and I will usually book a one-and-a-half or two-hour session. This time-frame is also driven by the fact that I am not on site in the way that most managers are, and I want to make sure that the sessions are complete; if the coach and coachee work in the same building, it is easier to reconvene or catch up between meetings.

At the beginning of a coaching relationship, meetings tend to happen more frequently – weekly, say – and then change to something like a fortnightly or a monthly pattern. This is because coachees tend to need more support in the early stages as they consider making changes and begin to implement them.

Reports of meetings

There are two main schools of thought that I know of in relation to reports of meetings. One school has it that the manager or coach should write up the meeting, the other that the coachee should. In both cases there is agreement that having a record of what was discussed and agreed and the action points is a necessity.

The argument for having the coachee write up the notes is that, in the writing, the coachee will achieve another level of clarity and responsibility. I think this works best when the coach is also the coachee's manager. When the coach is external and providing a service, then perhaps the coach should complete the meeting report.

I have taken to using a pre-printed sheet, like the one shown in Figure 8.2, which I fill in before the end of the meeting and then photocopy, leaving a copy with the coachee and keeping one for my own records. This pro-forma seems adequate for most needs.

Client	
Coach	
Meeting No	
Date	

Topics discussed:

....

....

....

Key Points:

....

....

....

Next Actions:

....

....

....

Next Session

Date: ....

Time: ....

Location: ....

Figure 8.2: Pro-forma report of coaching session

Chapter 9
Team coaching

In writing this book I have come to realise just how immense the topic of individual coaching is, and how it effects and is affected by virtually every domain of life. As we now get to the topic of team coaching, I am acutely aware that there is a new 'spin' on all that has been discussed so far, which adds a layer of complexity. I am talking about the obvious distinction between individual and team coaching: there are more people in teams.

At the surface level this means that more time is spent in the process of coaching. An individual can get to a level of clarity and make a decision relatively quickly. In a team environment, that process takes much more time as each person needs to be heard, each disagreement handled, consensus arrived at and commitment built. Now look beyond the surface – look at the interrelationships, dynamics and evolution of the team – and there is a whole new dimension.

I can genuinely say that the most exciting and fulfilling work that I have ever done as a coach has been with teams. This is because such work demands my full attention in every minute, and if I am working well I myself enter into the state of 'flow' that I described in Chapter 1. And I am a flow junkie. I will add that, despite all the complications and complexities, I do not think that we as coaches should find team coaching daunting. If the coach applies the basic rules of coaching and is fully focused and 'in flow', then the innate ability to coach will manifest itself, just as, in the ball catching demonstration described in Chapter 4, Peter discovered his ability to catch.

To do justice to the topic of team coaching would require a book bigger than this one. But it is an important application and, in my experience, a good one-to-one coach can transfer his or her skills to team coaching with time and practice. In order that this section can be most useful, the approach described is less about the skills and tools and more about what a coach can do to help a group of people experience being a team. In my view, of all the things that you need to know as a team coach, this is the most important. This is because when individuals come together as a real team they have less need of a coach!

The sections in this chapter cover:

- releasing the potential of teams
- the dynamics of teams
- techniques to reduce interference in teams
- using the GROW model in team coaching
- a typical team-coaching programme.

➡ RELEASING THE POTENTIAL OF TEAMS

Have you heard the one about the orchestra and the conductor? The analogy, that is. It is often used as an analogy for leadership and teamwork. The bit that sticks with me is the comparison of the conductor's role with the team leader's role.

I have to twist the analogy to talk about team coaching. Imagine a conductor approaching the rostrum, tapping his baton against the little reading light, clearing his throat and saying: 'Thank you. What music do you want to achieve today?' I would love to see the faces of the orchestra members. You see, this conductor is a team coach; there is no score, and the first task is to create one. The orchestra would be even more surprised if they knew that the 'conductor' knew next to nothing about music – but for a team coach, that is often how it is. He meets a team of people, facilitates the creation of a vision and then the development of a strategy, and helps the team agree roles and responsibilities and a *modus operandi*. The coach continues working with the team, learning with them, reviewing progress, resolving issues and drawing out creativity, inspiration and energy until the vision is achieved. And very often the team coach will not know very much about the actual work of the team.

All groups of people have the capacity to become teams, that is to say to achieve a mental state where they can give of their collective best. Obviously not all groups of people need to do that or are inspired to. The investment in becoming a team can be quite considerable. In organisations, particularly business organisations, it is important to balance the investment in building a team with the anticipated benefits. If the group has few shared goals and the goals that they do have can be achieved with ease, it probably does not merit spending significant time in building a team. On the other hand, if the group faces an almost impossible task that will deliver high value to the organisation – a task that demands all the team resources of skill and creativity – then investing in the team is desirable.

Here are three examples of groups of people that have different levels of being a team:

- *A work community.* This is a group of people who share the same work space and probably work for the same organisation. The tasks are probably not shared, and people have their own jobs and are not dependent on each other for their success. In a good work community, when one person gets bogged down or overloaded, others will help out. The need for a high level of relationship is low.

- *A working group.* This is a group of people who have a task that they share, such as a committee or working party. The task of the group is almost certainly only a small part of their job. They are dependent on each other for the success of the task but not for their overall success. The need for a high level of relationship is medium.

- *A team.* This is a group of people, usually small in number, who have shared goals and a common purpose for which they are collectively and mutually accountable. The goals typically demand the very best from the team. The need for a high level of relationship is very high.

A definition of 'team coaching' might be

The art of facilitating the performance, learning and development of a team.

This is the same as the coaching definition set out earlier in this book, with the exception of the last word. That word leaves many things unchanged but also changes others. The definition begs the question as to what is a team, and I am not looking forward to entering that particular minefield, primarily because the sense of being in a team is so different for each individual.

So let me ask a different question: What is the purpose in creating and maintaining a team? There can be only one answer: to achieve greater performance together than the individuals would apart. This in turn drives the question: what is it about being a team that gives greater performance? One of the places that the impact of being a great team is immediately noticable is in sport, and I can give a personal example here.

When playing competitive tennis at a junior level in Ireland, I joined up with another boy, Billy, whom I knew only slightly, to play doubles. He was from the north side of the City of Dublin and I was from the south side. Dublin is a small city but the north–south divide is miles wide. I had not chosen to play with Billy, nor he with me; the Tennis Association decreed that it should be so for the sake of the inter-provincial team. We played quite well together and even won a few tournaments, but there was something missing.

And then one day something different happened. I can still remember the exact moment, just as I remember the court and the people who we were playing. In the middle of a rally, without signal or spoken word, I just knew what Billy was going to do next and where he was going to move to. I noticed my body moving into open space to cover a shot without any conscious thought. The play became relaxed and spontaneous with the two of us moving in co-ordinated fashion, changing positions in a perfect and harmonious dance. When one made a mistake, there was no sense of blame or even frustration from the other, and there was as much joy in seeing your partner hit an awesome stroke as in doing it yourself. I never asked Billy if his experience had been the same as mine, for I did not need to.

This is an example of being a team. I know that it only involved two people, but many people report similar experiences from other activities involving greater numbers of people. So, what was it about being a team that gave greater performance? The Inner Game Model that I described in Chapter 1 – Potential minus Interference equals Performance – suggests that since our team was not playing to its potential then the first place to look would be to see what the interference was. All these years later I can identify a number of aspects of interference that may well have been getting in Billy's or my way – for instance, a desire to be playing with my usual partner, frustration at being forced to work with someone I had not chosen, fear of being judged, fear of letting the other down, not understanding how the other thought (and many more, I am sure). And in that rally we found 'relaxed concentration', a mental state in which we could perform to the best of our ability. What was different about this is that it was a shared mental state.

The purpose of creating and maintaining a team is to achieve higher performance. For a team to experience more of its potential, the interference must be reduced. Interference in a team might include:

- lack of trust in other team members
- fear of ridicule
- fear of being dominated
- pursuit of personal agendas
- a need to lead
- the pursuit of incongruent goals
- hidden agendas
- rivalries
- no listening
- no meaningful collective work
- fixed beliefs and positions ('This is how things are').

In contrast, a team that is successful in reducing the interference will be recognisable for:

- an apparent absence of hierarchy in the relationships
- robust, challenging conversations
- clear feedback sought and given

- the pursuit of 'impossible' goals
- focused activity
- an intuitive sense of where each member is and how they are doing
- requests made and offers given of help or support
- flexibility in roles and a willingness to cover for each other
- creativity, imagination and intuition as part of the toolkit
- team members caring for each other and their well-being
- fun, joy and the simple pleasure of being together
- silence and thoughtfulness before decisions and action
- mutual accountability for the achievement of goals.

If we consider team coaching from this perspective, then the role of the team coach is, in part, to help the team to reduce the interference and to achieve a team mental state. So the rest of this section of the book is devoted to that.

➡ THE DYNAMICS OF TEAMS

There is some really good news about coaching teams and, specifically, about reducing interference. It is this: most people want to be in a relationship with those around them, and they want the relationships to be meaningful. Now, they may have to unlearn some stuff before they can have those relationships, but at least as a coach you should know that, in this sense at least, you are working with gravity and not against it. There is something instinctive at work that guides people towards greater union. I do not particularly want to get spiritual about it but I guess it is a higher expression of what we are as human beings.

As a team develops and the individuals gain greater understanding of each other, the team passes through four distinct stages. There are two relatively well-known models that describe this process. The best known in the workplace environment is Forming–Storming–Norming–Performing, and a less well-known model is Pseudocommunity–Chaos–Emptiness–Community. Both these models have a lot to offer and are quite similar. The second model is from a book by M. Scott Peck called *The Different Drum*

(Rider, 1988). His book is about communities, not teams, but the process is similar.

Stage One: forming/pseudocommunity

When a team comes together for the first time, even if some of the members know each other, there is an unconscious game in play. The outcome from the game is that everyone should get on and that there should be no disagreement. The members play the game by a set of rules that preserves this balance and in order to preserve the balance, people pretend. They pretend that they agree with each other; they tell half truths and little lies. It is like being at a party with people that you do not know. 'Isn't the garden lovely?', another guest says. It's actually awful, and you both know it, but you hear your voice say 'Yes, they must work so hard on it.'

This is not the required atmosphere of a high-performing team, but it is where all teams start. In the workplace the ground rules are different but the game is the same. Everyone knows that George is manipulating the meeting, but the only time it gets mentioned is in the pub. Very little that gets said in the pub ever changed anything. In order for a team to be productive, it must move out of this pretence and get to a place where the truth can be told and where people can be all of who they are. But there are one or two steps on the way.

Stage Two: storming/chaos

Individual differences are not permitted in Stage One, but as the team sets about its task, differences will arise. As these surface, the team moves into a phase where disagreement, conflict and confusion prevail. The tendency at this point is often to retreat into Stage One again, with pretence coming to the fore.

Another thing that happens at this point is that the team members fight it out, trying to ensure that one version of the truth dominates, and team members try to convert each other to their own point of view. From this place, again no useful work can be done. The coach's job is to ensure that the team does not do that, but rather that it faces up to the differences. As the team coach, you need to be attentive to a typical response of teams to chaos.

They will blame you for it, thinking that you should have been a stronger facilitator.

Stage Three: norming/emptiness

This third stage is the most difficult for the team to tolerate. In order for the team to progress, the individual members have to be willing to give up on their version of the truth or reality or the right solution; they have to be willing to embrace another person's point of view, or even their right to have a point of view at all.

The second (Scott Peck) model is a more useful guide here. Teams will try to escape from chaos by imposing an order on things; they will establish project teams or sub-committees to come back with recommendations. That is all very well, but the team is still left with unresolved differences that are now probably even more difficult to get onto the agenda. The first model does not serve us well here, in that the danger of 'norming' is that it is simply another version of Stage One, pseudocommunity.

To move on, the coach works with the team so that the members listen to each other, acknowledge their differences and learn to look at issues from the perspective of another. A powerful technique to use when there is a conflict is to get one party to summarise the other party's position and then the second party does the same thing. It flushes out misunderstandings but, even more importantly, it forces each party to understand the other's point of view. When a team enters this third stage (emptiness in the Scott Peck model), it is as if all the interference evaporates and the team can enter Stage Four.

Stage Four: performing/community

The experience of this final phase can be very profound for the team. The team is there, fully present, and without a personal agenda or any attempt to win someone over. From here something magical can happen and the team can focus on its task. A place of creativity, insight and imagination has been found, where it is possible to see an issue as it really is. Decisions can be made clearly and easily, and a new vision created, with the full alignment of the whole team. The atmosphere amongst the team will be quiet, with a bubbling of joy and excitement just below the surface. One of the signs that the team is in this stage is the reluctance of the team members to leave a room when a meeting is over. This is akin to 'parting is such sweet sorrow' and should be indulged in.

Once the team has achieved Stage Four, it will carry that spirit with it for quite some time and will infect others that the members touch. However, the team will not stay in this space. The Stage Four will after a while become Stage One again and the whole process will recommence. Far from being bad news, this is *good* news. Each time the team passes through the four stages, the relationships deepen and become more resilient and trusting. The team – with help from the coach – also learns how to go through the stages, gets quicker at it and becomes more skilled in reaching 'team flow'.

There are two ways at least in which a coach can use this information. The first is simply to note the progress through the stages and let the model guide any required interventions; and not to panic when it gets tricky – the second stage is uncomfortable but essential. The second way is to reveal the model to the team and talk it through with them. This will give them some security in the second (chaos) stage and give them useful information on how to move forward. Sometimes, when I have spoken about the model and the team that I am working with gets stuck, someone will ask, 'Is this chaos?' And the very knowledge that it is allows them to persevere.

➡ TECHNIQUES TO REDUCE INTERFERENCE IN TEAMS

The coach can help a team identify and overcome interference in a number of other ways, and there are many techniques that can help. I have described a few below so that you can see some of the principles:

- generating a common vision
- identifying internal and external obstacles
- establishing ground rules
- disclosing life and career goals

- facilitating feedback
- bringing conflict to the surface.

Generating a common vision

Creating a common vision, or set of goals, can help to reduce interference inasmuch as it is tangible evidence that all the players are on the same side. The creation of the vision may also flush out disagreements about the direction the team is taking. A discussion early on in the life of the team that sorts out such differences reduces internal bickering and upset.

Creating a common vision can be approached in hundreds of ways. The simplest is to get each individual to write down their vision or goals; each person then reads out their vision. Other members of the team listen, and when the readings are complete the coach asks the team to identify the common points and themes. The advantage of starting with the personal vision is that the disclosure begins to generate understanding and therefore relationship within the team.

Identifying internal and external obstacles

This exercise is a way of getting the team to identify the interference for itself. There is more ownership that way. The question to ask the team is, 'What are the obstacles, within the team or outside the team, to your success, i.e. to your achieving your vision?' The coach will note down all the obstacles on a flipchart and have the team place them in order in terms of the impact on the team. The GROW model can then be used by the coach to resolve the issues, thus reducing interference.

Establishing ground rules

The potential for friction within a team can be greatly reduced by creating an agreement about how the individuals in the team will co-operate. The question for the coach to ask here is, 'What are the ground-rules that would support this team in achieving its goals?'

Start capturing the suggestions on a flipchart without engaging in debate or assessment. When the team has run out of suggestions, have them select those ground rules that they are all committed to. These should be reviewed at subsequent meetings and can obviously be changed, added to or removed.

Disclosing of life and career goals

This is a very simple exercise to perform and can even be done over a meal or a drink. Give the individuals some time to prepare and think through their goals – to do it properly the coach can work with the individuals prior to the meeting. The individuals then talk to the team about their personal goals. This exercise works because it builds understanding and, therefore, trust.

Facilitating feedback

I have already said something about feedback in Chapter 5. In relation to teamwork, the technique of facilitating feedback should again build understanding and trust in the group.

The simplest method is for each team member to take a turn in the 'hot seat'. The other members of the team then give the individual feedback. A standard format to the feedback can make this easier, covering (for instance) things the team members would like the person in the hot seat to stop doing, to start doing and (to give a full picture) to continue doing.

Bringing conflict to the surface

This need was touched on in the previous section on the four-stage models of the development of a team. There will almost always be a tendency to avoid conflict. If this happens the team is stuck and no meaningful work can be done. The coach's role is to notice the conflict when it rears its head and to ensure that the team talks it through.

Having the parties in conflict clearly state their position is the first step. Ensuring that the opposing party listens is the second. Another option, as described above, is to have each party state the opposing parties' position. As a coach, you also need to watch that the relationships survive intact or, better still, deepen as a result of the conflict. Questioning each party about how they feel about each other is a good starting point.

➡ USING THE GROW MODEL IN TEAM COACHING

Imagine you've just burst in on a team coaching session. It has already started and attendees have had a brief conversation around the topic for the day, but you haven't missed anything. This team is composed of the managers of the IT department in a bank.

Let me tell you who's in the room. On my left is Sally, then Tom, Peter, Jacintha and Frank. Frank is running the project. All the team report to me; some report through Frank. I have adopted the role of coach to the team, with their agreement. I think that's all you need to know to understand what's going on in Example 16.

Example 16: A team coaching session

COACH: Let me just check my understanding. As a result of our last meeting you went out and collected feedback from your internal customers. There are many good points in the feedback, like the quality of your solutions. The main area for improvement is in the quality of the service your provide. Is that correct so far?

PETER: Yes, pretty much.

COACH: Tell me what the specific feedback is.

TOM: The two main areas are that while the quality of most of what we deliver is seen as excellent, we are almost always late in delivery. In one particular case we were late by six months.

SALLY: Hold on. It's not that simple. The customer kept changing their mind.

PETER: Then you should have changed the delivery date.

COACH: It sounds like there might be something to discuss there, but let's not get into the detail yet. Tom, you said there were two areas for improvement.

TOM: Yes. The other area is that some of what we have delivered has not matched the customer's need. Now, in one case at least they did not discover this until the software was installed. And this is not a quality issue – the software works, but it just doesn't meet all their requirements.

COACH: Were there any other significant points raised in the feedback?

SALLY: I think that one thing people are asking for is more support in the hand-over of systems, and possibly for a short time afterwards.

PETER: You know we can't give that kind of support. We're short-staffed as it is.

SALLY: Well, it's what the customer wants.

COACH: Given all of that, what would be a useful goal for this session?

FRANK: I want to know what we are going to do about it.

COACH: Fine. So what would be a goal for the session?

JACINTHA: Maybe we could create an action plan to improve customer services.

TOM: We'd have to have an idea about what 'improved customer services' would look like – A vision or some goals.

PETER: That's all very well. But it seems to me that we've got a problem already. I'd like to understand that first.

COACH: I have heard three goals: to create an action plan, to have a vision or some goals, and to understand the current problem. Is that right?

FRANK: We could do all of that, I think. At least it's worth a try.

SALLY: OK.

COACH: Is everyone on board for the three goals?

VOICES: Yes.

COACH: Peter, what about you?

PETER: I think it's a lot to tackle. We always take on too much.

COACH: Are you willing to give it a go?

PETER: OK, but I'd like to start with examining the current problem.

COACH: Thank you. We've got our goals. And Peter would like to start with the current problem. Is that the best place to start?

JACINTHA: It's as good as any.

COACH: So what is the current problem?

PETER: The way I see it, certain people over-promise to the client. And that means that we end up not delivering what was expected, or being late. We have to manage the customer's expectations better.

COACH: When you say 'certain people,' who specifically do you mean?

PETER: Sally mostly, and sometimes Frank. Other than me, they are the only two people who agree work, so that has a big impact on the team.

SALLY: We keep having this conversation. I say that we should do everything we can to give the customer what they want – and even exceed their expectations.

COACH: That sounds like a pretty fundamental disagreement. Before we get into it, are there any other aspects of this issue?

JACINTHA: I think we are understaffed. We need at least one more person, a programmer.

FRANK: I believe that the budgeting process is getting in our way. We hold some of the budget and the customers another part. It makes negotiation very difficult.

COACH: So we've got a disagreement about what we offer the customer, a question about staffing and a budgeting issue. Which of these should we tackle first?

SALLY: I am tired of the battle with Peter. I'd like to get that out of the way.

COACH: Battle? That's a strong word.

SALLY: Well it's what it feels like. Every time we start up a project, Peter attacks me.

COACH: Have you told him that?

SALLY: I think so.

COACH: To be sure, why don't you tell him now?

SALLY: Peter, you are constantly attacking me over what you call 'over-promising' and I call 'delivering a great service'.

COACH: What is the effect of that on you?

SALLY: It's exhausting – and very frustrating. And, if I am truthful, I get quite upset about it.

PETER: I didn't realise. I'm sorry.

SALLY: OK.

COACH: I don't know if you guys need to do anything to restore goodwill or whatever.

SALLY: Maybe. Off-line. Later.

PETER: Yes. We can fix a time.

COACH: OK. And we are still left with the issue of what we offer the customer. I understand the over-promising part. What's the alternative?

PETER: You've got to manage the customers' expectations down. The budget is limited. There's only a certain amount of time and very often the technology isn't available.

TOM: I understand that, but my heart is with Sally. The job would become really boring if we just delivered the minimum. I need the challenge. I enjoy problem-solving and the opportunity to be creative.

SALLY: That's exactly what I think.

PETER: But if you do that, we all end up exhausted and constantly overstretched. And then you create more work by having to return to the customer to fix some part that didn't get dealt with properly the first time – more work.

TOM: Do you understand that that seems boring to many of us?

PETER: No. Well, of course. But don't think that I'm just some kind of boring bean-counter. I get satisfaction from delivering something that works.

COACH: Frank, where are you in this?

FRANK: I can see both points of view. I've just been thinking that what's going to matter in six months' time is what our customers think of us. Because when the new performance management system comes on line, that is how our performance will be judged.

JACINTHA: Can I say something? I don't think it matters whether Peter or Sally is right. I think that the customer is more important. I'm sorry to say this, but I sometimes think that Sally is so interested in the technology that she forgets the customer, and that Peter is so concerned about – well, how shall I say it – getting the balance between home and work right that he'll deliver the least he can get away with.

PETER: Another way of saying that is that Sally and I are concentrating on fulfilling our own needs and not the customers. Right?

JACINTHA: Maybe. I don't want to upset anyone.

TOM: It's an interesting point. What would have to change?

SALLY: We'd all have to focus more on the customer.

COACH: And what would that look like?

FRANK: Giving them what they want, what they really need.

COACH: How would you go about doing that?

SALLY: Spend more time talking with them.

PETER: Better analysis of the problem or need.

TOM: Being prepared to say 'no'.

COACH: Any other options?

JACINTHA: Involving them more in the development of the software.

PETER: I wonder – maybe on bigger projects – if we could get people seconded to our own team.

SALLY: The advantage in that, for the customer, is that one of their own team becomes the expert and they would be less reliant on us. And we would be certain to get a better understanding from each customer's perspective.

COACH: Any more thoughts? No. So which of these options do you want to take forward?

FRANK: All of them I think. But can we just hold off making a plan at this point. I'd still like to do the vision and that may alter the plan.

TOM: Good idea.

COACH: Ready to move on?

Now that you have read through the imaginary team coaching session in Example 16, have a go at Exercise 9.1 to analyse what can be learnt.

Exercise 9.1: **Using the GROW model in team coaching**

Purpose: To understand how the GROW model can be applied to teams.

Process: The questions are intended to be answered with reference to the team coaching dialogue of Example 16.

1 What do you notice that is similar between coaching an individual and coaching a team? List your suggestions.

2 What is different between the two? Again, list your suggestions.

3 What are some of the key skills of the team coach? List your ideas.

4 What techniques did the coach employ to manage the different ideas, perceptions and personalities in the room.

5 The 'atmosphere' in the team changes in the course of the session. Write down how you would characterise the shift?

➡ **A TYPICAL TEAM-COACHING PROGRAMME**

A team-coaching programme is likely to have many of the elements of an individual coaching programme. I say 'likely' because each situation is different and will have its own specific requirements. The programme outlined below describes the key elements.

Initial one-on-one meetings

If at all possible, a one-on-one meeting with each team member pays enormous dividends in terms of helping the coach understand the situation, design a programme to match the needs of the team, and build relationships with the individuals.

The agenda for such a meeting might include:

- an explanation of the purpose, goals and outline of the programme
- the team member's professional background and current role
- the team member's view of the 'current reality' of the team
- the team member's goals for the programme.

Initial team meeting

It is important to ensure that sufficient time is devoted to this meeting. On major projects, two days should be set aside for the team meeting as about the right duration. It is quite possible to break the agenda into sub-agendas to be tackled over a number of sessions, although the risk is that the team will not create relationships of sufficient depth.

Here are some of the key elements of the team meeting agenda at a very generic level.

- an explanation of the purpose, goals and outline of the programme and the purpose, goals and agenda of this initial meeting
- individual goals for the initial meeting and the programme, which should help craft the programme and agenda
- ground rules for the meeting
- The 'Current Reality', the intent being to generate an aligned view of the situation the team finds itself in
- a vision or project goals
- obstacles to achieving the vision
- key strategic levers
- an action plan
- a final review of the meeting.

Ongoing meetings

These should cover the following:

- a re-visit of the purpose, goals and outline of the programme
- a discussion of the purpose, goals and agenda of this meeting
- individual goals for the meeting
- a review of the ground rules for the meeting
- a review of the action plan from previous meeting
- coaching using the GROW model on priority topics
- an action plan

- a final review of the meeting.

If the programme takes place over a long period of time, it will be important to review progress in relation to the programme goals on a regular basis.

A final word of warning about team-coaching sessions. It is often the case that the team leader or manager is also present. If the prevailing culture in the organisation is authoritarian, or the team leader enjoys exercising his or her power, then the team and the leader need to understand that, to the degree that it is possible, everyone in the team has an equal voice. It is the coach's responsibility to ensure that and to run the meeting accordingly. Regular conversations with the team leader about the respective roles and the potential for conflict are recommended.

Chapter 10
Being a coach

This chapter is concerned with what it takes to be a coach. The previous chapters of the book deal mostly with the skills, models and tools of an effective coach. You can get results through becoming proficient in the use of those skills, models and tools, but this is far from the whole story.

There is a quote that I particularly like. It comes from a book called *What We May Be* by Piero Ferrucci (Thorsons, 1995), which discusses the subject of a particular psychology called psychosynthesis. In the book Ferrucci says: 'The way people act – what they produce and express and the way they relate to others – depends on what they are.' This part of the story is about *who you are as a coach* for, more than anything else, this will influence the quality of your coaching.

The diagram in Figure 10.1 will help to explain this notion. The circle on the right is the domain of Having; it is the results that you get. The results that you get are dependent on the actions that you take, represented by the domain of Doing. If you like the results then there is a tendency to repeat the actions that lead to it, whereas if you dislike the results then you are likely to do something different the next time around. (Actually, it is more complex than whether you dislike the results or not, and we will talk about that later in this chapter.) The actions that you take arise from your perception of how you see things. Your perception is a subset of who you are – the domain of Being, which includes your beliefs, values, attitudes, motivations and aspirations, as well as your particular psychological make-up and philosophy.

There are people in the world who are fit and healthy, and this is

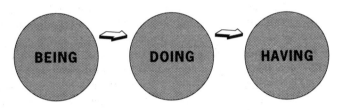

Figure 10.1: The source of results

a result they want in their lives. They get fit by doing certain things, like taking exercise and eating well. They do these things because – in their world, their perception – being fit and healthy is a good thing. If they took any other view, they would probably not exercise or care about what they ate. And they probably would not be fit and healthy.

As a further illustration, imagine a young sports person, say a golfer. This one has immense talent for the game. He has only one problem: he cannot seem to win the important games. Other boys with half his talent win more than he does. His father is the captain of the local golf club and has given our friend every assistance in his golf: the best equipment and tuition, and a willingness to drive him at all times of the day or night – no distance is too far – to play matches. His mother enjoys showing her friends the collection of silverware that her son has won.

Do not get me wrong, he enjoys his golf and occasionally gets satisfaction from playing well. He enjoys the limelight that he sometimes gets caught in, and he has a number of good friends and a great social life. Every time he stands up to hit a golf ball, he has more options than the rest of his peer group: he could hit the safe, percentage shot, down the middle of the fairway, that would please his father; he could play the shot that he has just seen in his mind's eye that is difficult but that he feels that day is well within his capability; or he could be completely outrageous and try to reach the green in one.

The trouble with the last option is that there is a stream just running beside the green. A kind of unconscious processing of all the options goes something like this:

- To keep Dad happy, I play the safe shot.
- To impress the gallery and my friend, I play the outrageous shot.
- To enjoy my golf, I play the shot I feel good about.
- To keep my friends, I fluff the shot (if I get too good they may not like me any more).

It is very likely that by the time he gets to play his shot he will not have made up his mind and will play a mixture of them all. In an unfocused state, he will certainly not play his best golf. Our friend is confused about *who he is as a golfer*. This will influence the decisions that he makes on and off the golf course. And will give him results that are well below what he is capable of.

Now tackle Exercise 10.1 to make your own assessment of the mindset of a coach.

Exercise 10.1:   **The Mindset of a coach**

Purpose: To identify the attitudes, values and beliefs of a coach.

Process

1 Write down some of the attitudes that a coach might have.

2 Write down some of the values that a coach might have.

3 Write down some of the beliefs that a coach might have.

As a coach, I have a point of view about an appropriate mindset. I want you to know that what comes next is *not* the truth; it is merely a proposition. I find that by holding on to this proposition and operating on the basis of it, I am a more effective coach. I will give it to you straight first, and then explain it in more depth:

- People have huge potential.
- People each have a unique map of reality and not-reality.
- People have good intentions . . .
- . . . and are achieving their own objectives – perfectly – at all times.

(These statements are adapted from a version that appears in *The Structure of Magic* by John Grinder and Richard Bandler.)

On first reading, you might find this a bit difficult to swallow. Let me take it statement by statement.

➡ PEOPLE HAVE HUGE POTENTIAL

Most people have a belief or a point of view about human potential. At one end of the spectrum you have the 'you can't teach an old dog new tricks' brigade; they are joined by the 'I am the way I am' and the 'Why do I bother?' brigades. They do not have much faith in human potential. At the other end of the spectrum you have the 'I can do anything I can dream of' brigade. When these guys are standing on a cliff flapping their arms in a frenzied imitation of a seagull, this is cause for concern.

I do not know where you stand on the spectrum; I just know you stand somewhere. I suggest that neither end of the spectrum is particularly healthy. The question that we should embrace as coaches is this: where on the spectrum should I stand as a coach, as someone committed to another's growth, development and full expression as a human being? In the story of Kevin, my assessment at the time was that the goal he had set himself was way beyond his reach. How wrong I was. To have taken the goal from him would have been to take away part of his life – a sort of well-intentioned murder.

Daniel Goleman, in his book *Emotional Intelligence* (Bloomsbury, 1996), states that late-nineties research suggests we are only using 0.01% of our mental capacities as human beings. Is that really so? I did the ball-catching demonstration that I described in the early part of this book at a small conference. The volunteer was a complete no-hoper, and I noticed myself making this value judgement in the first ten seconds, just in time to put it out of my mind. When the demonstration was over, the volunteer had surprised himself and the entire audience. I asked the group what they had noticed in the demonstration. The answer that silenced the room, and was the greatest acknowledgement I could have received was 'You believed in him, even when he didn't.'

➡ PEOPLE HAVE A UNIQUE MAP OF REALITY–NOT-REALITY

You have a mental map of reality. Much of that map was created in the first few years of your life and has not been updated since. You operate to a large degree on the basis of this map. If you think of a real-life journey you take regularly, you can probably visualise the route; you have a mental map of the route. A map, such as a road map, is a representation of the surface features of a territory in the same way that a menu in a restaurant is a representation of the food available. The menu is not the food; eating the menu will upset your stomach (and the waiter). Equally, the map is not the territory.

People, similarly, have a map of reality – but it is not reality; the way you think it is, is not the way it is. The way it is, is the way it is and does not particularly care what you think of it – it does not change for you. The fact that we have a map of reality (and not-reality) might not matter if all our maps were the same, but this is not the case. Each person's map is different – people have a unique map of reality–not-reality.

There are some people out there who think that the way they think it is, is the way it is. And when they say 'If I were you, . . .' they are actually just a little surprised that they are not you. These people do not make good coaches.

➡ PEOPLE HAVE GOOD INTENTIONS

I think that it is possible that in the world there is evil and that there are some people who are evil. I think of some of the monsters of history who perpetrated the most evil deeds. But maybe God whispered in the monsters ear and said 'Do this for me and do not question, because you cannot see the whole of my plan.' Maybe. However, most people – the very vast majority – have *good* intentions. They want to be happy and fulfilled and for others to be happy and fulfilled. They want good relationships with people. They want justice for all, the ending of starvation and hunger. They have good intentions in the big things in life and the small.

➡ PEOPLE ACHIEVE THEIR OWN OBJECTIVES

This morning, as I was writing part of this book, a neighbour told me that overnight someone had put a scratch-mark along the side of his car. It was done with a sharp object like a key. It means that the entire side of the car has to be resprayed. That represents quite a lot of money and a lot of hassle. He thinks that it was one of a group of youths who live at the other end of his road. On hearing the story, I was filled with righteous anger – kids these days! Hold on, though: my supposition is that people have good intentions and are achieving their own objectives, perfectly, at all times. It would be difficult to find the person who scratched the car and even if I could I suspect the answer to 'Why did you do that?' would be 'I don't know.' But maybe the youth was with his friends and scratched the car in order to gain acceptance in the group. And maybe he achieved his objective. This does not mean that there are no consequences, even unpleasant ones. It means that in the youth's map of reality the objective to gain acceptance had some priority.

Let me give you another example. I am thinking of the person who comes into work late and leaves early. She ignores the dress code and is surly to most of her colleagues, particularly those in management positions. Her work is badly done and seldom on time. The temptation is to conclude that she is a feckless layabout. That conclusion will help neither the manager nor the individual concerned. If a person has a position on a matter, then immediately and inevitably they create the opposite of that position; this is the nature of opposition. In opposition, there is no real dialogue. If the manager or coach approaches the workshy individual on the basis of personal value–judgements, then they will not have a meaningful conversation and nothing will change.

However, if the manager or coach engages on the basis that the individual has huge potential, has a unique map of reality, has good intentions and is, in fact, achieving her own objectives, perfectly, at that moment, then there is the chance for something to shift. Approach someone without judgement and with empathy and something special occurs; they may let you into their map of reality and, in sharing it with you, they may see reality differently and may choose to alter the map. I say 'may' because there is no guarantee. And empathy is a far stronger position from which to give feedback than condemnation. The apparently feckless layabout I told you about in the previous paragraph has an interesting recent history. She was offered a job in the department at a lesser grade than she had been on previously but was promised that the departments manager would be moving on in three months and that she was in line for the role. Then there was a re-organisation and the promise was forgotten. Now nobody knows what to do with her and her problem is shuffled backwards and forwards between her manager and the Human Resource Department. If you had not been willing to listen you would never have found out and to you she would always have been a feckless lay-about.

All this liberalism is all very well, I hear someone say, but it has not worked with young offenders or with single-parent mothers or whatever socially excluded group you choose to pick. The proposition does not say that people should be shielded from the consequences of their actions. People are responsible for the results they get in life. Liberalism and authoritarianism both have the tendency to remove responsibility from the individual. Effective coaching is empathetic but does not hide from reality; rather, it raises awareness of it and leaves the responsibility with the coachee.

A manager in an organisation is sometimes faced with a difficult choice: whether to invest time – and it can be a lot of time – in understanding a 'poor performer' or 'troublemaker', or whether to start disciplinary proceedings. And sometimes it will not be worth the investment.

The statements that make up this proposition were related to me by one of my first mentors, and I commend them to you even though they are not the truth. What they are is a powerful way of being a coach.

Self-awareness

Given that there is validity in the notion that who you are as a coach has a significant impact on your effectiveness, it follows that your awareness of yourself is a critical factor. Your understanding of your psychological make-up allows you to distinguish between an intervention that you might make to satisfy your own needs and one that will raise awareness for the coachee.

The goal is to be able to understand clearly what your intentions are in any intervention you might make in a coaching session. What exactly prompted that particular question? What was behind that bit of feedback? To make this real, let me take you out of the coaching context and bring you into my family. I am blessed with a step-daughter, Victoria. Both she and my wife are from single-child families; I, on the other hand, have three sisters and two brothers. My perception of what it takes to be a responsible, contributing member of a family is very different from that of Jo and Victoria. If my siblings and I did not do our share of the washing-up after dinner, then an absolute mountain of work would have been left for my mother; it simply was not an option to leave things for others to do. So sometimes when I see Victoria do something 'selfish', like leave the kitchen in a mess, it drives me crazy.

The point is that it is very often that my response has little to do with the reality of the situation and much more to do with my own expectations. It may be that it is simply easier for Jo to tidy up while Victoria gets on with her homework, and that they have agreed this. The same situation will occur in coaching. You as coach, will have expectations about how your coachee should behave that will have nothing to do with their reality. And even if you do not give voice to your expectations, the coachee will often pick up on them. Self-awareness is the well-spring of a non-judgemental approach.

In Chapter 11 I will talk about supervision and its role in coaching. For the moment, build the habit and practice of challenging yourself both during and after coaching sessions. Notice also how your coachees make you feel, for this will give you the clues you need to prompt further examination of your heart.

Intelligence, imagination and intuition

Having hit the warning note in the last paragraph, I am now in danger of appearing to contradict myself. I want to remind you that you are an experienced, intelligent, intuitive and creative human being. As such, you will have good ideas, observations and suggestions from which your coachees will undoubtedly benefit. Can you imagine being in a coaching session with someone who was completely stuck and having a good idea that you then withheld? Of course not.

The only criteria by which we can assess an intervention from a coach is through this question: 'Did it raise the awareness of the coachee?' If it did, then it worked. You have an important place in the coaching session – indeed, it is impossible that you would not have one because it is impossible to be completely non-directive. Just the unconscious raising of an eye-brow will communicate approval or disapproval to a coachee.

Letting go

Let me take you back to the insights of the Inner Game. The contention is that you have extraordinary potential. In this context, that means that you have extraordinary potential as a coach. That great coach that you can be is alive and well inside you and kicking to get out.

The model suggests that the way to releasing potential is to reduce the interference. It also suggests that the way to reduce interference is to get focused and achieve a state of 'relaxed concentration'. In this state, the ball-catcher catches the ball, Myles and Billy play a great doubles match, and Kevin plays his best tennis. In this state the innate coach will be manifested. You need to trust it, to trust yourself.

Where should a coach focus his attention? On the coachee. Not on the models, the techniques or the skills; not on whether the session will be a success or what the coachee thinks of you. These are all interference. Focus on the coachee. Get interested in their learning. Let go.

A wonderful gentleman, while learning to coach, came to a critical point in his own learning. He was trying very hard to get it right – to do it by the book – until he realised that this trying was getting in the way of putting his full attention on the coachee. In his next coaching session he focused on the coachee, and his and the coachee's experience of coaching was transformed; it became a fluid and seamless conversation. His comment afterwards was that the models and guidelines that we had been discussing up until that time were 'for the discipline of the novice'.

Chapter 11
Developing as a coach

This last chapter contains some ideas about how you can continue learning about coaching and how you can develop your ability and skills. As I indicated right at the beginning, this book cannot provide you with the most important part of learning to coach.

➡ PRACTISE, PRACTISE, PRACTISE

Use every opportunity you get to practise coaching, whether that be the formal and informal situations that occur every day at work, helping your children with their homework, or talking with a friend about a shared hobby or sport. Even in situations where coaching is not the appropriate approach, make sure that you listen in order to understand. Negotiations, meetings, dinner-time chat. Do this all the time and you will probably go mad; do it *some* of the time and you will become a better coach and probably a valuable colleague, friend, partner or parent. You will learn to coach by getting interested in other people's learning. Those you coach will be your greatest teachers.

➡ OTHER AIDS TO DEVELOPMENT

There are also some other routes to take, as set out hereafter.

Identify practice clients

'Practice clients' (who were mentioned early in Chapter 8 should be people who have a real interest in being coached but who know that you are in the process of learning. This gives you the freedom to make mistakes and seek feedback, while contributing to the 'relaxed' part of 'relaxed concentration'.

Co-coaching

Strike up an agreement with a colleague or friend who also wants to develop his or her coaching skills and swap coaching sessions. Remember, there should be no role-playing; you cannot learn to coach if the coachee can keep on making up new aspects to the situation. Choose issues, as the coachee, that if you could progress them would make a tangible difference to you.

In order to help identify issues for each other, you could ask the following to draw each other out:

- Tell me about a business goal that you are struggling with.
- Tell me about a problem you are having in work.
- Tell me about a skill you want to develop.
- Tell me about a vision you have for your future (in work or out of work).
- Tell me about a relationship in work that you find difficult.

Co-coaching works even better if there are three of you. One person is coach, another the coachee, and the third is an observer. It is the job of the observer to give feedback to the coach after the session. Watch that, in giving feedback, the observer restricts his comments to the coach's coaching and does not try to solve the coachee's problem. In one session, each person should have a turn in each of the roles. Coaching practice in threes has many advantages: the feedback; seeing coaching from three different perspectives; and being exposed to different approaches from each person.

Recording the sessions

Using video or voice recording of coaching sessions is a powerful way of raising the awareness of the coach. The temptation for the coach will be to watch what he did in the session; my advice is to watch the coachee even more closely, for that is where you will observe the impact of the coaching.

Feedback

Seek feedback ruthlessly. Finish each session with a request for feedback. If little is forthcoming, ask questions about the aspects of your coaching that you are concerned about. Make a list of the particular skills that you are focusing on and ask your coachees to rate you against them on a scale of 1 to 10.

Keep a diary

Keep a diary of your insights and learning as a coach. The act of writing has the effect of consolidating the learning. Be prepared to include learning that occurs in other areas of your life. Even note down your dreams – there is a potential wealth of learning there.

Get coached

If you want to learn to coach, get some coaching. What you learn at the receiving end – what works and does not work for you – is an invaluable source of learning. It is great if you can find someone to coach you who is talented, but you may find that you will learn just as much with a novice.

Undertake 'supervision'

When you have developed a certain degree of skill and are familiar with the models to the point that you have almost forgotten them, then you might turn your attention to the ways in which you unconsciously impact the coachee.

I refer you back to the piece, earlier in this chapter, on self-awareness. In the psychological disciplines, there is a practice known as 'supervision'. It involves one person overseeing the work of others. The intent, as I understand it, is to avoid the therapist's life and experiences becoming mixed up with the clients'. Supervision hardly exists for coaches, but I suggest that as the practice of coaching becomes commonplace so should supervision. It may be possible for you to find someone who is an experienced coach, who would be willing to perform the supervision role for you.

References and Further Reading

The Inner Game of Tennis by Timothy Gallwey (Jonathan Cape, 1975)
Coaching for Performance by Sir John Whitmore (Nicholas Brearley Publishing 1992 and 1996)
Emotional Intelligence by Daniel Goleman (Bloomsbury Publishing, 1996)
The Different Drum by M. Scott Peck (Rider, 1988)
What We May Be by Piero Ferrucci (Thorsons, 1995)

Index